Y0-CBG-535

OFFICIALLY
WITHDRAWN

Janice Horst Lucerne Valley
Branch Library
33103 Old Woman Springs Road
Lucerne Valley, CA 92356

THE
MOOD
BOOK

Crystals, Oils, and Rituals
to Elevate Your Spirit

THE MOOD BOOK

Crystals, Oils, and Rituals to Elevate Your Spirit

Amy Leigh Mercree

STERLING ETHOS
New York

STERLING ETHOS
New York

An Imprint of Sterling Publishing Co., Inc.
1166 Avenue of the Americas
New York, NY 10036

STERLING ETHOS and the distinctive Sterling Ethos logo
are registered trademarks of Sterling Publishing Co., Inc.

Text © 2019 Amy Leigh Mercree
Cover © 2019 Sterling Publishing Co., Inc.

All rights reserved. No part of this publication may be reproduced, stored in a retrieval system,
or transmitted in any form or by any means (including electronic, mechanical, photocopying,
recording, or otherwise) without prior written permission from the publisher.

This publication includes alternative therapies and is intended for informational purposes only. The publisher
does not claim that this publication shall provide or guarantee any benefits, healing, cure, or any results in
any respect. This publication is not intended to provide or replace conventional medical advice, treatment, or
diagnosis or be a substitute to consulting with a physician or other licensed medical or health-care provider. The
publisher shall not be liable or responsible in any respect for any use or application of any content contained
in this publication or any adverse effects, consequence, loss, or damage of any type resulting or arising from,
directly or indirectly, the use or application of any content contained in this publication. Any trademarks are
the property of their respective owners, are used for editorial purposes only, and the publisher makes no claim
of ownership and shall acquire no right, title, or interest in such trademarks by virtue of this publication.

ISBN 978-1-4549-3318-2

Distributed in Canada by Sterling Publishing Co., Inc.
c/o Canadian Manda Group, 664 Annette Street
Toronto, Ontario M6S 2C8, Canada
Distributed in the United Kingdom by GMC Distribution Services
Castle Place, 166 High Street, Lewes, East Sussex BN7 1XU, England
Distributed in Australia by NewSouth Books
University of New South Wales, Sydney, NSW 2052, Australia

For information about custom editions, special sales, and premium and corporate purchases,
please contact Sterling Special Sales at 800-805-5489 or specialsales@sterlingpublishing.com.

Manufactured in China

2 4 6 8 10 9 7 5 3 1

sterlingpublishing.com

Cover design by Igor Satanovsky
Interior design by Christine Heun

To my beloved twinsie, Jamie,
the most supportive soul sister
a girl could ever have.
And to the goddesses of light
who guide my steps and unfurl my creativity
with their supernatural midwifery.

INTRODUCTION

The *Mood Book* is all about you. It's like your own personal mood ring. It wants to know how you are feeling and how can it help. It's organized into easy-to-follow sections based on your mood. If you're anxious, you will find baths, suggestions for essential oils and crystals that can help, and guided meditations to help you find your Zen. If you have a big presentation coming up at work and you need to shore up your confidence, you will find the perfect physical exercises and metaphysical suggestions to rock your career. If you're feeling sensual and romantic, you will find the perfect essential oils that will enhance the mood, colors that will accomplish different objectives, and the subtle spiritual meanings of different flowers that can be used for romantic healing and benefit.

This volume is sequenced around five different groupings of types of mood, and it provides suggestions for bettering each mood. It shares powerful and fun self-care rituals, delightful quizzes, metaphysical tools of the trade that can help you accomplish your objectives, and ways to optimize your life and environment.

I've been a medical intuitive and life coach for the past seventeen years. I have heard from thousands of clients about what they struggle with in their day-to-day lives. This book is a fun and entertaining way to address all of those women and men and provide easy, uplifting, actionable steps to feel better now. Because that's what we all want to feel good and live a positive life. *The Mood Book* will teach you how.

HOW TO USE THIS BOOK

Here is a guide to help you navigate all of the fun and fragrant tools in this book. We will discuss how to use essential oils, charge crystals and much more. So, let's dive in!

All About Oils

How to Use Oils

Not everyone is going to like the smell of every essential oil, so it is important to get an idea of what you like before you decide to buy. Liking the smell is extremely important here because in this book the oils are being used to influence mood. Think about it this—if you buy a perfume or aftershave because it's the trendiest scent at the moment, but you don't really like it, how often will you wear it? With essential oils the same is true. Take some time to find the scents that you like, even if it whittles your list down to only two or three.

Diffuser

Essential oil diffusers are a good option. Diffuse the oils for about half an hour at a time and then switch the machine off. Half an hour of exposure to the oils in this manner will deliver an adequate dose of tranquility.

Mobile Therapy Unit

Make your own mobile therapy unit by getting a small bottle that seals properly and that has dark sides. Fit in a cotton ball and then drop in your essential oils. Leave it in the glove compartment of your car, in your desk drawer, or in your purse, and open the bottle to take a whiff whenever you need to.

This should last for a few months, but if you find that the scent is fading, change out the cotton ball and add more oil. Use the diffuser to help you stay calm when you're in a traffic jam, waiting on a line, or need to stop anger in its tracks.

Body Lotion and Perfume

You can make a lotion using essential oils—use a quality aqueous cream base and mix in a few drops of the oils you choose. Feel free to mix and match a little to create your own blends, not just the ones suggested in this book. When experimenting, use a small dollop of cream and a drop of each oil. If the end result smells pleasing, you've hit on a winner. You could also mix the oils into your normal moisturizer or body lotion. Alternatively, mix them into a carrier oil like sweet almond oil or coconut oil and massage gently into your temples, shoulders, and neck as necessary.

Basic Lotion/Oil Recipe

1 cup aqueous cream

Up to 20 drops of your choice of essential oil

Place everything into a clean container that can be sealed and stir thoroughly. Apply as needed.

All About Crystals

How to Use Crystals

There are a variety of ways to use crystals. For serenity, it is best to use a combination of crystals in your environment and carry crystals with you. You could use the crystals to focus on during meditation or consider using them as gem essences.

In Your Environment

This is an extremely effective way of changing the energy in a particular area. Place a stone on your desk where you can see it, or place a larger stone in each corner of the room. If you want a more peaceful night's sleep, you can put the stone next to your bed, under your pillow, or under the mattress.

Use as a Touchstone

This is where you keep a stone on you at all times and are able to touch it whenever you need to. The advantage of a touchstone is that you don't need any specific jewelry setting. All you need is a pocket or little bag to keep it in as you go about your day.

All the stones in this book make good touchstones, and this is an ideal way of using those that need direct skin contact.

Jewelry

This can be a convenient way of using the stones. If the stone, like black tourmaline or carnelian, is best used against the skin, it is best to use it in the form of a pendant or ring where the stone can touch the skin.

Healing Layouts

This is where you lie down and place the stones on the chakra points (energy vortexes) of your body, or surround your body with the stones. There are many different healing layouts that are effective, so explore and experiment and find the best one for you. You can also use clear crystal points to boost the effectiveness of any of the crystals listed in this book. Simply lay out your crystals according to your chosen selection and then hold the clear crystal point above the area, with the point facing your crystals. Clear crystals boost the effectiveness of other crystals when used in this way.

Gem Essences

This is where the crystal is placed in a glass of distilled water and left out in the sunlight or moonlight. The water then contains the essence of the gem and can be ingested or used for bathing. When making gem essences, be careful about which stones you use.

You do not want to use any soft stones as these might dissolve in the water and leave traces of toxic minerals.

Remember that you need to know exactly what the stone you have is. If you have a pure citrine crystal, for example, that's simple enough. But what about stones where there is more than one type of mineral present? Do you know exactly what the stone contains? Here it is best to do copious research and err on the side of caution. So, if you are not sure whether or not it is safe to use a crystal to create a gem essence—just use it in another way.

How to Cleanse and Charge Crystals

Crystals act as conduits for energy, which is the reason that they are so helpful when it comes to healing. The downside is that the more they are exposed to negative energy, the more negative energy they absorb. This means that every so often, it is necessary to cleanse the crystals of all the negative energy contained within and recharge them with positive energy. This is a simple enough procedure and should be done after every healing session or after you have been carrying the crystal around for the day.

Here are the main ways to cleanse and charge your crystals. As you will see, each of the main elements—earth, air, fire, and water—is represented.

Using Water

Ideally use a natural spring, if you can get to one, but tap water will also do. Allow the crystal to be submerged and feel the negative energy being washed out of it and down the drain. This should not be used for crystals that do not do well in water, like opals and sapphires. When the crystals are clean, set them out in direct sunlight so that they can dry naturally. (This has the added advantage of charging them as well.)

Using Earth

Burying crystals in the earth, like leaving them in the sun has the dual purpose of both cleansing them and charging them. Look for a patch of earth that is relatively dry and leave them in there for at least an hour, preferably overnight. When you dig them out, use a soft cloth to dust them off if necessary.

Using Incense or Dried Sage

Choose incense that you like and light it. Pass the stones through the smoke a few times. This is called smudging.

Using Sunlight

If you are short on time, you can place the crystals in the sun for a few hours, and this will help cleanse them as well.

Using Moonlight

Some crystals, such as Amethysts may change color when exposed to the sun. In these cases, cleansing them in moonlight is a viable alternative. Other crystals just love the moonlight. The full moon is good, but not essential. Leave them overnight.

Using Salt

Salt is an extremely potent cleanser and will draw the negative energy out of the crystals. Use plain, untreated sea salt and bury the crystals in it overnight. If the crystals are softer and so more prone to scratching, do not use this method.

Using Sound

This can be effective, especially if you need the crystals cleansed in a hurry. Clap cymbals together right next to the crystals so that the sound waves pass through them. Alternatively, you can place them in a Tibetan singing bowl and bring it up to the right frequency. If you are using this method, do take care that the stones are not fragile or brittle, because they could be damaged by doing this.

All About Plants

How to Use Plants

Herbs can be used in many different ways. Tea infusions are a popular and effective method. Plants are also used for their medicinal and aromatherapy properties in different spa treatments, remedies, and even floral arrangements. There are many overlapping uses for each of the herbs and plants listed in this book.

In Teas

A tea is actually an infusion unless you are making it with a variety of teas, such as white green, or black tea. To make an herbal infusion, simply soak a dried or fresh herb in hot, warm, or boiling water for a period of time to extract some of its medicinal properties. Some infusions are premade in teabags. You can also place chopped herbs in a muslin bag or in a metal mesh container to soak them in hot water. Many teas are better made with water just a bit cooler than boiling. Some herbs are delicate and will retain more medicinal qualities if they are not exposed to water that is vigorously boiling. Herbal infusions are best consumed warm, not hot, so let them cool a bit first.

Steam Inhalation

Steam inhalation is a lovely way to take in the goodness offered by some herbs. Infusions can be made to create steam for inhalation. You can do this with a large bowl. Make sure it is not metal or made of something that will be dangerously hot to the touch once you've added hot water.

Add the steaming water and the herbs to the bowl. Carefully place a towel over your head and get close to the steaming water. Use caution as you approach it and wait until the heat is comfortable and you can breathe in the vapors without burning your face.

You can even breathe in the steam from a hot, steamy cup of herbal tea. That delivers a bit of healing vapor with a small amount of effort. Another easy way to inhale botanical goodness is to place a few drops of essential oil on the floor of a steamy shower (but not near where you're going to stand). You can also place dry aromatic herbs in a satchel and position the satchel under the hot water as you shower.

TURN
WORRY
TO
PEACE

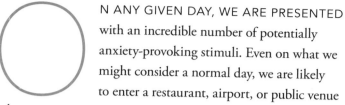

O N ANY GIVEN DAY, WE ARE PRESENTED with an incredible number of potentially anxiety-provoking stimuli. Even on what we might consider a normal day, we are likely to enter a restaurant, airport, or public venue where we encounter one or more televisions presenting us with frightening or disturbing imagery and commentary. Nowadays, people seem to have normalized this level of highly stimulating media. And although it may have become the norm, it does not necessarily mean that it has a positive effect on any of us.

Studies have shown that exposure to twenty to thirty minutes of violent imagery is proven to depress the immune system for up to thirty days. It's likely that many people are operating with a constantly depressed immune system due to regular consumption of aggressive media. There's a part of us that always wants to turn up the volume to seek and consume more stimulation. This is not wholly negative. Sometimes, amplifying and activating certain systems can be a good thing. But at times it comes at the expense of our inner peace. Our job is to strike a balance.

In this section, we will explore all kinds of ways that you can turn worry into peace. We will talk about essential oils that can help you de-stress and revitalize, discuss inviting and serenity-filled rituals that you can prepare for yourself, and examine which types of minerals and crystals can help you invoke a sense of tranquility. Finally, we will indulge in a relaxation ritual. So, gently wade into the warm and embracing waters of inner peace that are beckoning you on the following pages.

Anxiety-Soothing Oils

You have the power to alchemize your mood. Even on days when events outside of your control feel like they are getting you down, you always have the opportunity to go home and regroup and revitalize. You have an extensive toolkit at your disposal with mental, emotional, physical, and spiritual resources to be used to improve your quality of life.

Let's talk about those days when we feel anxious. Maybe we're nervous about an impending breakup or getting back behind the wheel after a car accident. Perhaps we feel overstimulated in our fast-paced world. We are tethered to our electronic devices by choice, endlessly consuming media that has given us as a society a 1,200 percent rise in the diagnoses of anxiety disorders since 1980. Sixty-six percent of all adults suffer from nomophobia—fear of being without a mobile device. Forty-eight percent of people report lying awake at night due to stress. Something needs to change.

Essential oils have earned their place in history because of their powerful ability to make us calmer and feel more serene. They are uniquely useful when it comes to inducing a sense of calm and peace because they work at a physical and emotional level.

QUESTION 1

I am stuck in rush hour traffic, so I:

1. Sit back and relax—there is nothing I can do about it anyway.

2. Get out of my car and try to see what is going on.

3. Honk the horn out of sheer frustration.

4. Freak out completely because I will once again be late for work.

QUESTION 2

I have just seen my child's costly phone bill, so I:

1. Sit down for a bit to let myself calm down.

2. Call the company to check if there are any errors.

3. Throw it down in a fit of frustration.

4. Tell my child to get downstairs immediately.

QUESTION 3

**My boss just took full credit for
one of my ideas again, so I:**

1. Feel annoyed but realize that there will be another chance for me later on.

2. Moan to a co-worker about it.

3. Storm out of the meeting.

4. Corner the boss and let them know what I think of them.

Add up the numbers of each answer you chose to get your score. For example, if you chose answer 4 for question 1, you will have 4 points for that question.

If Your Score Is 10 to 12

It sounds as though you are very stressed and could use a break. If you cannot take some time out, the following essential oil blend will help you calm down quickly and efficiently:

* ✳ **2 drops of vetiver oil:** This is a deeply scented oil that soothes the mind instantly. It smells warm and earthy.
* ✳ **2 drops of sandalwood oil:** This oil is redolent of summers spent playing in the woods and has just a touch of an exotic undertone.

Use in a diffuser or in a mobile therapy unit pages x–xi).

If Your Score Is 7 to 9

If you fall into this category, your problem is more simple frustration than outright anxiousness. However, if you do not start taking steps now, it could escalate into feelings of anger.

Take the time to start relaxing more by taking walks in nature or trying meditation.

Look at the following blend to help ease frustration and bring your mind into a calmer more relaxed state overall.

* ✳ **2 drops of ylang-ylang oil:** This will help to soothe frustration and leave you feeling calm. It is also a great idea to use this oil if you are battling to sleep at night because of emotions you are processing.

✳ **2 drops of frankincense oil:** This oil has been used since ancient times to help aid meditation and promote calm and understanding for the spirit.

Use in a diffuser or in a mobile therapy unit (see opposite page). You can also dilute this blend in a carrier oil, like jojoba or coconut oil, and then apply it to your feet and legs before bed for an exotic and relaxing dose of aroma and calm.

If Your Score Is 5 or 6

Congratulations! You already have some serenity in your life and are not likely to fly off the handle at any second. But there is always room for more relaxation. This blend gives the body an opportunity to avail itself of deeper rest and restoration.

　✳ **2 drops of lavender oil:** This will soothe any irritated feelings and help you feel calmer and centered.

　✳ **2 drops of chamomile oil:** Chamomile is great to use if you are battling to fall asleep because there are too many thoughts whizzing through your mind.

Use in a diffuser or in a mobile therapy unit (see page 4). You can also dilute this blend in a carrier oil, like jojoba or coconut oil, and then apply it to your feet or massage into your scalp and temples before bed for relaxing dose of peace. Keep it away from your eyes, nose, and mouth.

If Your Score Is 3 or 4

Well done—you don't really need much help from the Serenity Fairy, do you? Your focus should be on furthering that sense of calm through meditation and improving mindfulness. This blend will help you bring greater presence to your life so that you can experience peak performance.

    ✳ **2 drops of neroli oil:** This will make it possible for you to relax and enjoy the bliss of the moment.

    ✳ **2 drops of jasmine oil:** This will help you keep your focus and build your confidence at the same time.

All the Oils You Should Consider for Serenity

    ✳ For complete relaxation: vetiver and sandalwood.
    ✳ For meditation: ylang-ylang and frankincense.
    ✳ To reduce anxiety: lavender and chamomile.
    ✳ To improve serenity and lift mood: neroli and jasmine.

Of course, this is only a guideline. Do yourself a favor and find a place where you can test these scents. There will be some that smell rich, like vetiver, and others that smell more exotic, like ylang-ylang.

Here are a few recipes you might enjoy.

Lavender Fields Body Oil

1 cup apricot kernel oil

10 drops lavender oil

5 drops chamomile oil

5 drops ylang ylang oil

Mix all the ingredients together and then massage them into elbows, feet, and especially areas of dry skin spots.

Sleep Tight Lotion

1 cup aqueous cream

10 drops sandalwood oil

10 drops lavender oil

Place everything into a clean container that can be sealed and stir thoroughly. Apply as needed throughout the day.

Bye-Bye Tension Rub

1 cup aqueous cream

10 drops vetiver oil

5 drops frankincense oil

5 drops sandalwood oil

Mix all the ingredients together and then massage them into tense spots.

Tension-Go Salt Rub

1 cup sea salt

1 cup Epsom salts

5 drops neroli oil

5 drops chamomile oil

5 drops jasmine oil

Mix together all the ingredients and keep them in a sealed container overnight before using them. You can use this as a relaxing salt scrub in the shower to start or end your day.

There are many easy ways to start incorporating essential oils into your daily life. Use the oils to help keep you feeling more centered or to help you meditate more completely. It is completely up to you—where will you start?

Tranquility Crystals

Crystals have been used for centuries to promote serenity and as a tool for meditation. They can be helpful allies in our quest for calm. Minerals and stones hold unique properties that can induce a sense of tranquility.

Smoky Quartz

This is an outstanding option if you have baggage from the past holding you back. It is also good for when you feel you are in a rut or the energy around you has started to stagnate. Keep it with you consistently to help get rid of resentment and negative energy and to feel at peace.

Citrine

Citrine is the ideal crystal to help you get up and seize the day. It helps to restore confidence and will help you build a more prosperous future. It is also good protection against negative energy, so keep it on you at all times.

Larimar

One look at this stone and you start to feel at peace. It is the best option when you have swirling emotions and mood swings. It also helps improve your intuition and makes it easier to make rational decisions.

This stone is also famous for being able to create a feeling of peace and tranquility in all who see it. Some people feel a connection to dolphins when using this stone. It is believed to be associated with those loving and benevolent mammals.

You should keep larimar separate from other stones—it is softer than other stones and can easily be scratched.

Blue Sapphire

Blue sapphire is sacred to the god Saturn. Where possible, look for stones that have a lighter blue tone, as these are more effective. These stones help to restore peace of mind and protect you from danger.

Wear these as jewelry for good luck and to keep nerve-racking incidents at bay.

Amazonite

This stone is very soothing. If you are feeling anxious, all you need to do is to touch it, and you will feel calmer. It is also a good stone to meditate over, especially when you are feeling guilty, remorseful, or cynical. It is also excellent for releasing blocked emotions.

Blue Lace Agate

This stone is the perfect spiritual stone for meditation. It is excellent for calming the nerves, especially if you have a propensity for being hot-blooded. It has a gentle cleansing energy.

Rose Quartz

If you only choose one crystal on this list to help ease your mind, make it rose quartz. This is a powerful stone that helps you reduce stress and feel true contentment. It is the best stone for restoring compassion and is excellent at clearing negative energy. This stone is all about unconditional love.

Carnelian

One of the most popular stones in ancient Egypt, carnelian will help you completely relax. It also brings about a higher feeling of contentment and can help you make the right decisions. If you want lasting and complete inner peace, this is the stone for you.

Topaz

This stone is also deeply relaxing and grounding. If you have been battling to let go of grudges, this is the right stone for you. It helps to balance the emotions and can be worn as jewelry.

Black Tourmaline

This is a protective stone that is excellent for dispelling negative energy from the home. If placed underneath your pillow or mattress, it will help promote peaceful sleep. If you feel someone is trying to hurt you, wear the stone for protection. It restores peace of mind and serenity by being a very grounding stone.

Condition	Stone	Best Way to Use	Charge With
Release of emotional baggage	Smoky quartz	Carried on you	Sand/moonlight/ sun/water
Motivation	Citrine	Carried on you	Sand/moonlight/ sun/water
Relaxation of the consciousness	Larimar	Carried with you	Moonlight/ water
Peace of mind	Blue sapphire	Worn	Moonlight/ water
Reduction of anxiety	Amazonite	Carried with you	Moonlight/ sun
Meditation	Blue lace agate	Carried with you	Sand/ moonlight/sun/ water
Contentment and peace	Rose quartz	Carried with you	Sand/ moonlight/sun/ water
Relaxation	Carnelian	In direct contact with your skin	Sand/ moonlight/sun/ water
Expression of your desires	Topaz	Wear as jewelry	Moonlight/ sand/ water
Peace of mind after being wronged	Black tourmaline	In direct contact with your skin	Sun/ moonlight
Clarification of decisions	Bloodstone	Carried with you	Sand/moonlight/ sunt

Bloodstone

Bloodstone is an excellent helper when it comes to restoring serenity of mind and thought. It helps you to clarify your purpose and make difficult decisions.

It is an incredibly grounding stone that helps you feel present in your body. It is also useful for clearing away dense and heavy energy. If you use it for that purpose, it is important to clear the dense energy from the stone afterward. Placing it in the sunlight and moonlight for 24-72 hours should do the trick. Ideally outside, preferably on the earth. In a pinch, a sunny windowsill will work.

Peaceful Plants and Herbs

The world is full of countless species of plants, herbs, and flowers that have been used to tackle a range of diseases and health concerns since before recorded history. It's incredible to discover the medicinal benefits available to us through plants and herbs. Many of the "solutions" brought to us by the pharmaceutical industry borrow names, ideas, and methods of action from these ancient medicinal plants.

Many of their uses that are not discussed in depth here include other medicinal benefits that are more specific to physical health concerns, such as treating digestive issues and inflammation, promoting healing, and many more. Plants, herbs, and flowers can produce increased feelings of serenity, happiness, love, romance, courage, confidence, and vitality. These effects have been experienced by humans throughout millennia and used by many different societies all over the world. We'll discuss the myriad benefits and uses of herbs and flowers including mental health, clarity, relaxation, self-esteem, boosting energy, and so much more.

These herbs and flowers can be used for different intentions that can help you achieve a state of serenity. The most common way to use these herbs is in teas, but many can be used in various other ways.

BASIL *(Ocimum sanctum/Ocimum tenuiflorum)*

Basil is known to be an antidepressant. It has a stress-relieving effect and is calming. It can be beneficial for relieving anxiety and can be used to make relaxing teas. It is traditionally thought to be a sacred herb. Its leaves and flowers are medicinally useful. Infusions can be made to create steam for inhalation. This can soothe stress, relieve congestion, help you overcome uneasiness, and enhance relaxation.

GREAT FOR: *Stress, relaxation*

VALERIAN *(Valeriana officinalis)*

Valerian promotes sleep and has been used historically in different cultures to treat nervousness. It is considered a tranquilizer and has been shown to depress the central nervous system and relax muscles. It can help overall physical and mental health and has been used to treat irritable bowel syndrome, asthma, muscle tension, restless leg syndrome, and different phobias. It assists in total body and mind relaxation, most importantly decreasing stress and anxiety and promoting proper sleep. Valerian was used in wars to treat nervous stress and shell shock. It is recommended to use it only at night, as it does have a strong sedative effect, and not to mix with any other pharmaceuticals. It can be steeped in tea for 15 minutes or taken in a concentrated extract form.

GREAT FOR: *Sleep, anxiety*

LAVENDER *(Lavandula officinalis)*

Lavender is a popular flower that is said to have antidepressant, relaxant, and central nervous system actions. It has been traditionally used for its relaxing and calming qualities. In fact, some studies show that using lavender in aromatherapy can decrease the presence of the stress hormone cortisol. Lavender has been used to relieve insomnia and depression in combination with other medicinal herbs. In studies, lavender has been proven to be more effective than pharmaceuticals in assisting patients to get a restful sleep. Dried lavender flowers can be placed inside a pillow to encourage relaxation before, during, and after sleep. In some parts of the world, burning lavender is used to smudge and purify areas. Dried lavender flowers are often hung in rooms for relaxing aromatherapy and because they are also known to repel insects. Lavender is also used to clean and soothe skin. It can be infused into creams, soaps, and other body treatments to incorporate healing and relaxation to your self-care routine.

GREAT FOR: *Relaxation*

CHAMOMILE *(Chamaemelum nobile/Chamomilla recutita)*

This flower is known to be incredibly soothing and a great way to treat anxiety. This is because it is considered a sedative and relaxant. It is a popular tea that is often sold in single-use tea bags but can be created by simply steeping the dried flowers without any additional treatment. It is also beneficial to use the cooled tea as a skin-healing face wash. Infusions can be made for inhalation or other body treatments. Chamomile is a popular herb used for a wide array of healing intentions. It is sometimes referred to as an "herbal aspirin."

GREAT FOR: *Anxiety*

THYME *(Thymus vulgaris/serpyllum)*

This herb has a long history, inspiring poets and providing medicine to many. It treats a number of physical ailments through its antibiotic, antiparasitic, antiviral, and expectorant actions. In aromatherapy, it is used to alleviate symptoms of exhaustion and depression. Women experiencing symptoms of premenstrual syndrome or individuals experiencing stress may also benefit from thyme in aromatherapy. This can be as easy drying thyme and leaving it in common spaces or creating infusions to use for inhalation in steam. Thyme is a very versatile medicinal herb that is able to help the body release sickness and prepare for experiences of serenity.

GREAT FOR: *Stress, meditation*

VERVAIN *(Verbena hastata/officinalis)*

Indigenous communities in North America have used vervain medicinally for centuries, if not longer. It treats many ailments with a sedative action. The herb can be infused to make a tea that alleviates insomnia. Vervain can also be used to make tinctures, which are known to be helpful in treating exhaustion and depression.

GREAT FOR: *Depression, exhaustion*

ST. JOHN'S WORT *(Hypericum perforatum)*

This wild herb has a lot of history and has recently regained popularity in its use for treating nervous conditions. It's considered a sedative and antidepressant, and it's important to not take it in combination with any other antidepressants, as it is believed to increase levels of serotonin in the brain. Taking this herb can help to treat anxiety, depression, nervous tension, irritability, and other emotional upsets. It is also known to be beneficial in treating symptoms of premenstrual syndrome and menopause. This herb is often taken in the form of a tincture for a minimum of two months to treat nervousness and depression.

GREAT FOR: *Anxiety, irritability, PMS*

SKULLCAP *(Scutellaria lateriflora/Scutellaria baicalensis)*

This herb has many historical uses by indigenous tribes of North America. It is a sedative and is used to soothe anxiety, nervous exhaustion, and tension. It has many restorative properties that assist the body and mind in nourishing the central nervous system, calming overall levels of stress, and relieving feelings of anxiety. It also assists in relaxing the body through its antispasmodic action, which is very beneficial for individuals who experience body tension caused by stress and worry. Due to its sedative effect, it is also used to treat insomnia and other sleep disturbances. A tincture created from fresh skullcap herb is the most efficient method for easing nervousness, but capsules and tablets are also effective. It is often mixed with other herbs to treat certain ailments. A great tea for sleep mixes ½ teaspoon each of skullcap, passionflower, lemon balm, and spearmint. Let this recipe steep for 20 minutes before consuming.

GREAT FOR: *Tension, stress, worry, sleep*

SCHISANDRA *(Schisandra chinensis/Schisandra sphenanthera)*

This plant is indigenous to China and Korea and produces different types of flowers and berries, depending on the type of plant. Outside of these areas, it is not very well known, but studies have shown that it is a very effective adaptogenic herb. The medicinal value is found in the berries. They contain vitamins C and E, and they can produce sedative and anticonvulsant effects. The berries are believed to be able to treat depression and reduce irritability. It is also said to stimulate breathing and concentration, so it could also be used as an aid to reach deeper states of meditation. Chinese medicine believes these berries can "calm the heart" and also "quiet the spirit." To use this plant medicinally, the berries are traditionally chewed or can be processed into a tonic or tablet.

One of the traditional uses is as a supplement to stave off hunger and to help improve energy levels. The berries are usually dried to preserve them. Just be warned: they really do not taste very good, so it is better to find an extract.

Schisandra will help protect your body from the negative effects of stress, improve endurance and stamina, and reduce mental fatigue as well.

GREAT FOR: *Meditation, depression, irritability*

ROSEMARY *(Rosmarinus officinalis)*

Doctors in medieval times believed that anxiety could be treated by placing rosemary under a person's pillow at night. Throughout history, this herb has been used to treat depression. It is administered safely via ingestion, via inhalation, and as an ointment. It is also a great herb to mix with chamomile and sage to create an herbal hair rinse, as rosemary is known to give hair strength and a beautiful shine. This herb is linked to lowering levels of the stress hormone cortisol. It can be used via aromatherapy by placing the dried herb throughout your space or by simmering a pot of the herb on your stovetop to fill your home with the scent. You can sip on rosemary tea to produce calming effects and only need a small amount. For ingestion, a little goes a long way.

In addition to using rosemary under your pillow, you can create a necklace or a medicine pouch to keep the herb on your person. You may use the necklace as aromatherapy whenever you are beginning to notice you are feeling stressed, overwhelmed, or simply searching for a moment of meditation or serenity.

GREAT FOR: *Anxiety, depression, stress, meditation*

ROSE PETALS *(Rosa)*

Historically, rose petals were valued for their medicinal qualities more than their aesthetic qualities. Rose has antidepressant properties. It can be consumed and used in teas, steams, and compresses, and its seeds can be ingested. Inhaling rose steam vapor helps to induce sleep, and it is often combined with other flowers or herbs. Certain species of rose bloom are used for women's perfumes. These same species have been known to be used medicinally in treating depression and anxiety.

GREAT FOR: *Depression, sleep, anxiety*

PASSIONFLOWER *(Passiflora incarnata)*

This plant is known to treat insomnia, nervousness, headaches, and hysteria. It also assists in reducing anxiety and high blood pressure. It acts on the central nervous system and therefore should not be used with antidepressants. It is considered a tranquilizer and sedative and can be used to treat mild pain. Passionflower tea is very popular in Mexico to relax and for sleep. Tinctures are used to calm anxiety and restless minds. Tablets are also commonly sold for stress and insomnia. The flower is a gorgeous addition to any home and lovely when worn in your hair.

GREAT FOR: *Sleep, anxiety*

SAGE *(Salvia officinalis)*

Sage is a calming plant. There are many different species. Depending on the strain, sage can be used to make infusions for hair rinses or to create a calming tonic for stress or menstrual pain. It is a great herb to place in flower arrangements. It can be dried and included in homemade soaps and body scrubs, among many other home beauty remedies.

GREAT FOR: *Nervous tension, anxiety*

Worry Less Bath

After a long day, it's natural to feel wound up and stressed out about the week ahead. The idea of going to sleep can seem like a steep climb into restlessness. Are you worried you said something humiliating that you can't live down? Do you have a case of imposter syndrome—that feeling that you're not good enough to have your position at work, your current relationship, or your general place in life? It may do you some good to prepare a serenity bath ritual with natural mood boosters like essential oils, candles, and herbal tea, while practicing mindfulness and visualization with pretty rocks.

Gather the following materials:

* Paper
* Pen
* One or more pieces each of moonstone, clear quartz, "phantom" quartz, amethyst, lapis lazuli, and larimar
* Lavender essential oil
* Valerian essential oil
* One pastel-colored candle of your choice
* Chamomile tea
* Dried lavender
* Lavender soap (optional)

Prepare a cup or pot of chamomile and lavender tea, with a 3:1 ratio of dried chamomile flowers and dried lavender (found at health food stores). Chamomile tea is a gentle and common decaffeinated herbal tea that boasts a long list of health benefits. It contains alpha-bisabolol, which settles the symptoms of irritable bowel syndrome and gastrointestinal inflammation. The other key active ingredient is apigenin, a bioflavinoid that eases anxiety and helps with sleep. Infused with lavender, which has pharmacological benefits that also fight anxiety, depression, and insomnia, this brew will put you at ease for the rest of the night. Take long, mindful sips as you prepare the bath; don't just chug the tea without appreciating its flavor profile and warmth.

Begin running the bath. When the tub fills a little bit, add a couple drops each of lavender and valerian essential oils. If you have a diffuser, add drops to it as well and turn it on near the bathtub. Smelling and tasting lavender at the same time will have a therapeutic grounding effect and ought to activate your highest (crown) chakra. Lavender is said to encourage pleasant, introspective dreams. By contrast, valerian, which is much harder to find in the form of an essential oil, opens up the throat chakra and thyroid glands to absorb spiritual energy. Both scents have a calming effect on the central nervous system, leaving you feeling less irritable when getting ready to bathe or sleep.

Take a minute to think of some positive, reassuring affirmations to write down on a piece of paper. Your emotional goal should be the pursuit of inner peace and serenity. For example, think of the well-known Serenity Prayer with a divine feminine variation: "Great goddess, grant me the serenity to accept the things I cannot change, the power to change the things that I can, and the wisdom to know the difference." You can remind yourself that everything is going to be okay and that everything happens for a reason, especially because you're about to use powerful spiritual tools to lift you out of worry. Think about the positive energy hanging in the air that you will harness to elevate your mood and sense of well-being. Trust that any persistent, invasive thoughts disappear with the steam wafting off the bathwater. Visualize yourself solid and stable like an oak tree, not uprooted by strong winds.

Once you have a meaningful statement written down, put the piece of paper in a place where it won't fall into the bathtub, but where you will clearly see it throughout your soak. Then, light your pastel candle and repeat your affirmation, mantra, prayer, or positive visualization as you ignite the wick. Place the candle near the piece of paper, but be sure it will not set it on fire. Start undressing and dimming the bathroom lights, and turn off all your devices so that nothing interrupts the serenity ritual. Slip into the warm water and get comfortable. Gather your crystals and rest them on the edge of the bathtub, within arm's reach.

Start by using your piece of larimar, a light blue stone mined only in the Dominican Republic. This rare variety of pectolite is most potent in rebalancing the throat chakra, concentrated in a band of energy around your neck, ears, nose, and mouth. When your throat chakra is out of whack, your communication skills suffer; you might not know how to articulate yourself, or you might overexpress yourself in hostile, accusatory ways. Listening and talking to other people should be a socially fulfilling experience that doesn't create unnecessary stress, so if a barrier seems to exist between you and the rest of the world in this way, the problem could literally be stuck in your throat.

A lot of frustration, anxiety, and unhappiness are propelled by negative self-talk. In social situations, we may think that we aren't good enough or that others are judging our actions under a microscope, when usually those thoughts couldn't be farther from reality. When the throat chakra is clogged, it's hard to quiet self-deprecating themes entering the mind. Our deepest insecurities reinforce themselves in a toxic feedback loop, polluting our inner monologue.

Envision your throat chakra opening up under the soothing, pastel blue glow of the larimar's vibration. Place the rock on your throat over your vocal cords, take deep breaths in and out, and hum. Set the intention to speak your truth and live your truth—to be bold and brave. At the same time, pledge to open and unclog your ears so that you may actively listen to the other person during a conversation. Most important, invite divine coincidence into your life: believe that individuals come into your orbit for a reason, and hope that you always end up in the right place at the right time. In the most vital moments, your wit and intelligence will shine through.

The reassurance emanating from the pale blue larimar on your throat will overlap with that of the darker blue aura of the lapis lazuli, which is to be placed on your third eye (brow) chakra. Sometimes flecked with gold, this stunning metamorphic rock can be pricey, but it is effective in bringing peace and serenity to the mind's eye and your vocal cords. Alternate between these two chakras when using lapis lazuli to maximize its power. Physically, the rock is said to alleviate headaches and sore throats, along with general inflammation.

Lapis lazuli's great value comes from the wisdom it carries from ancient civilizations like Egypt and Mesopotamia. Let the guiding spirits stored in the rock adjust the view of your third eye so that it is open just the right amount to receive life's deepest messages. Hold on to the crystal while meditating to deepen your focus and feelings of tranquility. In this moment, find solace in your now-sharpened sense of intuition, and be kind to yourself when memories of past failure come up. You are the greatest version of yourself that has ever existed, and in the future, your best attributes will only become stronger personal qualities.

For the part of your ritual that incorporates quartz, be sure you have a clear quartz wand, which does not have to be fancy. This basic metaphysical tool amplifies other energies and intentions that are placed within it; hold this crystal on your brow bone and visualize positive outcomes for situations in your life on unsteady footing. Remind yourself again of your strong intuitive powers and wish to see life from a widened perspective.

Try to get your hands on a piece of quartz with a "phantom" that appears when held up to a light. The appearance of a crystal within a crystal like this brings the owner courage. Linked to the development of one's intuition, phantom quartz signifies the not-fully-realized parts of one's character that are bound to grow and develop. The "phantom" symbolizes this ideal version of yourself and your commitment to becoming a better human being. Through your mind's eye, focus like a laser beam on your unfinished characteristics, watering them like plants with optimism and hope.

Move on to your trusty piece of amethyst, which, like quartz and lapis lazuli, works on both the third eye and crown chakras. More than anything, amethyst is a transformer stone: it helps people break bad habits and fixes situations so that they are not as devastating. You might be engaged in destructive patterns that bring you anxiety, but you can call on your amethyst stone to invigorate your willpower and endurance to break these patterns. As you rub the amethyst all over your forehead, ask it to chase away nagging, addictive thoughts. Picture its soft purple aura surrounding you with eternal self-love, wrapping you in a cocoon from which you will emerge as a butterfly.

Finally, pick up your heavy-hitting piece of polished moonstone, thought by many to unlock one's "inner goddess." Its properties correspond to the lunar cycle, to feminine energy (regardless of one's gender), and divine love. Put the opalescent stone atop your head, rubbing it all over your skull. Pray that your body's internal systems are working rhythmically, like the ebb and flow of the ocean tide. Let the nurturing maternal energy of the moonstone center you and remove aggressive impulses; think about the need to actively listen instead of arguing one's point. Practice love and understanding in all that you do, and look for bits of yourself in other people when you have trouble humanizing their behavior. Find the serenity now to believe and act as though everything will find its place in the universe, and pledge to practice patience in all future conflicts. Locate a source of love from a higher power, such as the moon.

Line your crystals up along the side of the bath. Wash yourself with lavender soap. Don't worry about shampooing and conditioning your hair; just make sure your body is clean and pure. While finishing up your bath, practice gratitude for the tea, the sweet essential oils, the crystals, and the bathtub itself. Even as you step out onto the bath mat and wrap yourself in a fresh towel, relish the texture of the dry fabric. You'll feel refreshed, revitalized, and markedly less anxious and stressed out than you were earlier. The ritual ensures you get an amazing night's sleep, as well. Sweet dreams!

Restful Sleep Ritual

We all know how bad we feel in the morning after not
sleeping properly the night before. But is it really such a
terrible thing to miss an hour or two of sleep here and there?
After all, there never seem to be enough hours in the day, so
perhaps it makes sense to cut down on time wasted sleeping.

This couldn't be farther from the truth.

The Effects of Sleep Deprivation

The problem with sleep deprivation is that the effects are
cumulative. If you have missed out on as little as one or two
hours a night over the course of a few nights, the effects are
the same as if you didn't sleep at all.

At best, your productivity levels will drop, you will be
more prone to making mistakes, and you will not be able to
react as quickly as normal. At worst, you might experience
periods of microsleep. This means falling asleep, even for a
short while, while going about your day. This is fine if you
are relaxing on the couch, but not so great if you are driving
your car. The physical effects can be just as serious. Sleep
deprivation has been linked to an increase in obesity. There
are two reasons for this. For starters, if you are tired, you
are less likely to be active. Second, your levels of leptin and

ghrelin are likely to fluctuate. This, in turn, leads to you feeling hungrier and eating more. Because you are fatigued, you are more likely to reach for high-calorie snacks that give you an instant rush of energy.

How Much Sleep Is Enough?

Clearly, it is important to get enough sleep. The actual number of hours will vary from person to person. It is recommended that adults get between seven and eight hours sleep a night.

Am I Getting Enough Sleep?

There are two easy ways to tell if you are getting enough sleep or not. First of all, how long does it take you to fall asleep at night? It should take around fifteen minutes or so in someone who is not sleep deprived. If you fall asleep as soon as your head hits the pillow, it is a good indication that you are sleep deprived.

Another easy way to tell that you are sleep deprived is that you have to rely on an alarm clock to wake you every day. That is not a good sign—your body is designed to go through several phases of sleep at night and should be able to wake itself up naturally.

Can't I Just Catch Up on the Weekend?

Unfortunately, no. In fact, sleeping in on a Saturday and Sunday will be doing a lot more harm than good because it upsets the circadian rhythms of the body. As already noted, your body should be able to wake itself up naturally. This is due to circadian rhythms which are your body's natural processes that cycle about every twenty-four hours.

How Do I Reset These Rhythms?

It can be easy to upset the sleep cycles of your body. If you do, you will suffer for it in the long run because you will not get tired at the right time and not wake feeling refreshed. Resetting the rhythms takes time but is a matter of routine.

You need to create the same routine every day before sleeping and on waking. That means going to bed at the same time every night and getting up at the same time every morning. If you miss bedtime one night, do not be tempted to try to sleep in the next day, but rather get back to your normal routine as soon as possible.

Good Sleep Hygiene

Before we discuss a sleep ritual that will help you get a refreshing night's sleep, we need to talk about good sleep hygiene.

Good sleep hygiene means making the conditions in your bedroom as conducive as possible to sleep. That means banishing all electronic screens—no TVs, no tablets, or phones. No phone? Yes, I hear you gasp in horror at that one, but it is worthwhile. Skip endless updates on social media and get a better night's sleep. You will be thankful in the morning.

The problem with electronic devices is that the light they emit simulates daylight. This, in turn, prevents the production of melatonin, the hormone that helps us to feel sleepy.

While we are on the topic of light, also remove anything that has an LED light anywhere on it and install dimmer switches on your main lights. About two hours before bedtime, switch off all electronic devices and dim the lights.

A big part of getting a good night's sleep rests in ensuring that your bedroom is dark enough. Consider installing blackout blinds or wearing an eye mask if your bedroom is light at night.

Make your bed a haven for sleep. Start by choosing the right mattress and pillows. You want a mattress and pillow that are comfortable but that still offer you the right support and keep your spine in proper alignment all night. For example, if you mainly sleep on your back, you want something that has a little more firmness to it, so that you don't sink all the way down into the mattress and leave your neck at a funny angle. Or, if you sleep on your side, choose a pillow that has a slightly higher loft so that your neck stays straight when you are sleeping.

Choose good-quality bed linens. Natural fibers are best, because they allow air to circulate around the body. This aids in temperature regulation and allows you to get a better night's sleep overall.

You can also improve your bedtime experience by spritzing your sheets with a linen spray in the morning when you make your bed. A lavender linen spray is perfect because it smells lovely and will help calm the mind and let you drift off to sleep. As you uncover the bed to climb in at night, the scent will be wonderful, and this further reinforces the notion that your bed is a haven for you.

Several linen sprays are available on the market, but these often contain harmful chemicals. And, while several claim to contain essential oils, the actual quantity of the essential oil is usually quite low.

These artificial sprays may smell very nice, but they have no actual therapeutic value. They might even be doing you harm because they are so loaded with chemicals. It is easy enough to make your own linen spray free of toxic chemicals.

Making Your Own Linen Spray

20 drops lavender essential oil (therapeutic quality and preferably organic)

250 ml water (distilled is better, but any water will do)

50 ml cheap vodka (optional; helps the oils disperse in the water)

Place all the ingredients into a clean spray bottle and mix well. Shake each time before using. You can spritz your sheets with the mixture just before pulling up the covers.

You could also spritz the sheets with the mixture just after washing them, when they are almost dry.

Your Guided Sleep Ritual

Step 1: Start Winding Down

Routine is your friend here, because it enables your body to start acting on autopilot. You want to establish a ritual that signals your body that it is time to go to sleep. Dimming the lights and switching off electronic devices is the first part of that routine.

In the couple of hours before it is bedtime, do tasks that are not mentally challenging—find an easy book to read, for example.

Step 2: Do the Legs-up Yoga Pose

This pose is considered passive and thus does not require any special dexterity or fitness level. This pose has several benefits:

* It is deeply relaxing: Because you are in a semi-prone position and have slowed your breathing, your body's relaxation response starts to kick in. Your heart rate slows and you start to feel more relaxed in general.
* It helps improve circulation and promote the drainage of lymph: Lifting your legs up like this improves the flow of the liquids in the body—lymph, water, and blood—toward the heart. Gravity actually assists in pulling the liquids down from the feet and lower legs.
* It relieves swelling of feet and ankles and alleviates pain: This is the perfect move to counteract the negative side-effects of either sitting or standing all day long.
* It stretches out your hamstrings and lower lumbar region: Your hamstrings are bound to be tight after a long day sitting behind a desk. This move stretches the hamstrings gently so that they can loosen up. It also stretches out the muscles in the lower lumbar region.
* It eases tension in the back: This move takes all the pressure off your lower back, and so it can be useful in relieving strain.

✳ **It relaxes the pelvic floor:** Your pelvic floor opens up in this pose, and this allows it to relax.

Doing the exercise is simple enough. All you need to do is to position yourself on your back, facing a wall. You can either choose to get down onto the floor or lie on a bed.

Position yourself a few inches from the wall with your legs resting up against the wall, but not quite at a ninety-degree angle. If you like, you can place a cushion under your pelvic region before you get started. You can rest your arms straight out in a T or at your sides. You want to feel really comfortable in this position.

Lie back and do some deep breathing. It doesn't have to be anything complicated. Just breathe in for a count of five, hold your breath for a count of five, and then breathe out for a count of five.

Stay in this position for five to ten minutes. You should feel your body relaxing and muscle tension melting away. Make sure get up slowly and take your time until you feel fully present and ready to reenter your day.

Step 3: Your Intention Journal
Start by finding three to five things that you were grateful for during the day, things that made you feel good, and make a note of these. This is useful because it helps to remind you of all you have and helps elevate your thoughts and feelings. This, in turn, is helpful when it comes to getting a restful night's sleep.

Once you have written that down, write down an intention. This is similar to an affirmation but is designed to set you up for a good night's rest. Do not be tempted to skip this step, because it can be a very powerful one.

Just before going to sleep, think about how well you will sleep and how refreshed you will be in the morning. The next morning, even if you do not get as good a night's sleep as you would like, you will wake up feeling better. The mind is extremely powerful, so harness that power to your advantage by setting your intention before bed.

Choose a phrase that resonates with you, something like, "My sleep is deep, rejuvenating, and serene. When I awake, I feel refreshed." This should be the absolute last thing that you do at night before switching off the lights.

With this ritual, you will find yourself enjoying a much more restful sleep immediately. If you continue performing the same ritual every night, it won't be long before your body gets used to the routine and your sleep patterns improve.

TURN SADNESS TO JOY

E ALL EXPERIENCE LIFE'S UPS AND downs in different ways and in different quantities. Sometimes we have a great month and everything flows smoothly, and sometimes there's a lot of change or turmoil in our lives. But through these ups and downs of life that are inevitable, we have an opportunity to bring our focus on a daily basis to the transformative power of joy. I believe joy is the highest vibration in the known universe. As a medical intuitive for over fifteen years, I have seen joy's healing power in action. Joy has the power to raise the vibration of the cells in our bodies. It has the power to raise the frequency of the energy in our bodies. Our bodies are amazing wonders capable of self-correction and self-regulation. Joy is one of our most essential energetic nutrients.

In this section, we will explore all kinds of ways that you can turn sadness into joy. We will talk about essential oils that can help you tap into your own inner wellspring of happiness. We will share enticing and joy-filled rituals that you can prepare for yourself. We will explore which types of minerals and crystals can help you invoke a sense of bliss. We will also learn about different plants and flowers and ways that you can use them to promote boundless joy. Then, we will meditate together to cultivate bliss. Finally, we will indulge in a joy ritual together. Let's dive into the ocean of bliss together.

NOTE: Your mental health is crucially important. The flip side of happiness can be depression. Clinical depression is a very real mental health challenge and should be treated by a qualified professional. There are times when these issues are far more challenging than just thinking positively. The problems can be chemical based or stem from major psychological challenges. This book is not meant to take the place of psychological or psychiatric care. It is simply a booster, guide, and support. You matter, and if you are dealing with major challenges like depression or anxiety, please find the help you need so you feel good again.

Happiness Oils

Have you been feeling a little down lately? Perhaps not sad but not bursting with joy either? In this chapter, we will look at essential oils that can help you to feel blissful and euphoric again.

If your get-up-and-go got up and left, take this quick quiz to see which oil is best for your particular situation.

QUESTION 1

Think back to the last time you felt truly happy. How would you describe it?

1. Must I only choose one time?
2. It was a few months ago, but the details are still pretty clear.
3. It was such a long time ago, I have forgotten.
4. I don't remember ever being truly happy.

QUESTION 2

I would be happy if I didn't have so many worries. I worry:

1. Worry? What's the point? It just makes life more miserable.
2. In stages. I try to limit myself so that I don't become one massive ball of worry.
3. Quite a bit. You never know when something is going to blindside you.
4. All the time, over things that haven't even happened yet.

QUESTION 3

Happiness is:

1. A state of mind. I can choose to be happy.
2. Out there. I just need to work on finding it.
3. Possible if only things would go my way.
4. Something that I never seem to get a chance at.

Add up the numbers of each answer you chose to get your score. For example, if you chose answer 4 for question 1, you will have 4 points for that question.

If Your Score Is 10 to 12

It sounds as though you may be depressed and might consider giving yourself the gift of some caring, professional help. The following oils will help put you in a sunnier frame of mind, but please also take action to make sure your experience of life is a positive one. You matter, and you are worth the effort.

* **2 drops of jasmine oil:** Jasmine is one of the few oils that can invoke feelings of ecstasy just by sniffing it. It does have a strong scent but will leave you feeling calmer and a lot happier. (It's also a bit of an aphrodisiac.)
* **2 drops of bergamot oil:** This is one of the best oils for those suffering from depression.
* **2 drops of rose oil:** Rose is an oil that has such a wide range of uses that it doesn't come as a surprise that it is included here. It will help you to manage your emotions and gently uplift your spirits.

If Your Score Is 7 to 9

You are definitely in a joy deficit. It is important for you to put your attention on cultivating joyful experiences in your life every single day. If you make a commitment to joy, you will attract more of it. Whatever you put your attention on is what will get done, so, if you decide that you are going to find fun, blissful, pleasure-inducing experiences for yourself every day, more will start showing up in your life even when you are not trying to find them. Essential oil therapy can be very effective in uplifting mood.

* **2 drops of neroli oil:** This oil buoys your spirit. It also aids sleep that is impaired as a result of feelings of sadness.
* **2 drops of cedarwood oil:** This scent was used during ancient times. It helps to balance mood and leaves you feeling calmly focused.

If Your Score Is 5 or 6

You have a fair amount of joy in your life already, but there is always room for more. Boundless, endless bliss and joy are good goals!

* **2 drops of lime oil:** Citrus oils all have excellent mood-lifting properties and can have you feeling lighter in no time. Lime oil is useful in dispelling sadness. You can also squeeze a bit of lime in your water to encourage your liver to gently release any stored energy of sadness.
* **2 drops of ginger oil:** Ginger is most commonly known for its ability to settle the stomach. It also enlivens the mind. The combination of the two make for a scent that is plainly divine—it is like sunshine in a bottle.

If Your Score Is 3 or 4

You have the right attitude. Happiness is more about how we view our circumstances than what those circumstances actually are.

* **2 drops of grapefruit oil:** This helps you to put some more pep in your step and helps you to feel livelier.
* **2 drops of nutmeg oil:** This will give you a whiff of the comforting smell of baking and holidays and help you feel more relaxed and positive.

All the Oils You Should Consider for Happiness

* For gloom: jasmine, bergamot and rose oil.
* For mild depressive states: neroli and cedarwood oil.
* For when you need a little lift: lime and ginger oil.
* To maintain a great mood: grapefruit and nutmeg.

It is important for you to go out and see which of these scents appeal more than others. For example, maybe you won't like the somewhat cloying scent of jasmine and prefer the cleaner tones of the grapefruit. You'll get a sense when you start trying the oils.

If only one or two of the oils on this list make it into your shopping cart, don't worry about it—simply introducing a new scent, as long as it is one that you love, can help to improve your mood tremendously. In fact, it is a lot more important that you love the smell, because then using the oil evokes positive memories and associations. As a general rule, any of the citrus oils will work well if you have the Monday morning blues—they help with depression and boost energy levels.

Here are some recipes to get you started.

Bliss-Inducing Perfume

- **1 cup sweet almond oil**
- **3 drops cedarwood oil**
- **7 drops jasmine oil**
- **5 drops neroli oil**
- **5 drops ylang-ylang oil**
- **5 drops rose oil (optional)**

Place everything into a clean container that can be sealed and stir thoroughly. Apply a little to each wrist and the neck as you would with your normal perfume.

Euphoric Scrub

- **1 cup sea salt**
- **1 cup Epsom salts**
- **10 drops jasmine oil**
- **5 drops rose oil**
- **5 drops cedarwood oil**

Mix together all the ingredients and keep them in a sealed container overnight before using them. Mix into a little carrier oil and smooth over your skin just before showering.

Happiness Facial and Toner Spray

- **1 cup distilled water**
- **⅛ cup witch hazel**
- **10 drops bergamot oil**
- **10 drops grapefruit oil**

Mix everything together and spritz your face as needed.

Room and Linen Spray

1 cup distilled water

2 tablespoons witch hazel or vodka (helps the oils disperse in the water)

10 drops lime oil

10 drops ginger oil

Mix everything together and spritz in the room as needed. I find that spraying the curtains and lampshades helps to ensure that the scent lasts most of the day. You could also spritz the laundry just before it is completely dry or when you are going to iron it. With essential oils, there are many different ways to lift your mood. Start by choosing the ones that you like best, and you will see just how powerful these oils can be.

Ecstatic Crystals

Crystals can be used to lift your mood and make you feel happier. Stick to crystals in sun colors for the very best results.

Yellow Apatite

If you have been finding yourself feeling somewhat glum, this is the perfect stone to help improve your mood. It boosts your sense of self-esteem and helps you feel more hopeful again. It makes all things appear possible and inspires you to be more creative.

Yellow Jasper

All varieties of jasper are grounding, and yellow jasper is no different. The biggest plus with this stone is that it gives you a renewed sense of optimism. It works at a deeper level to bring more positive things into your life.

It helps to reduce stress and will leave you feeling happier, even if you started off feeling down. It is one of the best stones for fighting depression.

Charge it in the sun to enhance its positive aspects to their fullest.

Citrine

This is a stone of plenty. It can create abundance in your life in many different forms. Use the stone to manifest the life of your dreams and to help you adopt a more positive attitude. It is also helpful in relieving the of stress of having too much to do.

Use it in conjunction with amethyst to give you peace of mind and boost your levels of optimism.

Sunstone

This is one of the best stones to use to lift sadness and restore feelings of self-worth. If a negative self-image is at the root of your problem, start carrying a sunstone or wearing sunstone jewelry.

Just looking at the sparkling inclusions within the stone can help you to feel happier.

Aragonite

If you are battling to be happy because you feel overwhelmed by problems, this is the kind of stone that you want to invest in. Place it against your forehead to help clear your mind or place it over the solar plexus to help calm your nerves.

Condition	Stone	Best Way to Use	Charge With
Improving your mood	Yellow apatite	Carried on you	Moonlight/sun/ smudge
Relieving depression	Yellow jasper	Carried on you	Moonlight/sun/ smudge
Creates abundance	Citrine	Carried on you	Sand/moonlight/ sun
Feelings of sadness	Sunstone	Worn	Moonlight/sun/ smudge/sand
Dealing with problems	Aragonite	Carried on you	Moonlight/sun/ smudge/sand

Plants for Glee

Many of the herbs and flowers associated with happiness overlap with those found in the other sections. Happiness is a sensation that can be accessed when we feel calm, serene, and confident. We can cultivate a state of bliss when we are able to let go of stress, worry, and distracting thoughts. We can feel joy and euphoria much more easily when our body and mind are in a state of ease.

ROSE PETALS *(Rosa)*

Rose petals can have a positive effect on mood by lifting spirits and opening the heart. This beautiful flower is said to have more than three hundred chemical constituents, of which only roughly one hundred have ever been identified. There are many species of roses, each with varying medicinal uses. Roses are known to have antidepressant actions. One way to use this herb is by inhaling steam with rose and other herbs, as this has been known to create feelings of happiness and ease. Rose petals are also dried to create teas. You can steep a tea with rose petals and receive the benefits of aromatherapy as you smell your delicious tea.

GREAT FOR: Joy

CHANNA *(Sceletium tortuosum)*

This herb has been known to create joy for those who use it. It is consumed traditionally by chewing the leaves. It has also been consumed by snorting the crushed leaf powder or smoking the herb. Today, it can also be consumed as a supplement in gelcap form. When smoked, it is known to enhance mood and social skills. This method is also known to reduce anxiety and stimulate feelings of lightness and happiness. In large doses it creates intoxication similar to cannabis or other psychoactive plants. The intoxication usually involves being able to laugh more easily and general feelings of joy and euphoria.

GREAT FOR: Euphoria, joy

DAMIANA *(Turnera diffusa)*

Damiana has been used historically by ancient civilizations and continues to be used today. It has many effects that can promote feelings of happiness, joy, and euphoria. It is known for its antidepressant and aphrodisiac qualities. You can consume it by drying the leaves of the herb and then infusing them to make a tea or a steam for inhalation. Inhalation of this herb's vapors in large quantities has been reported to produce more intense feelings of euphoria. Overall, it promotes feelings of comfort and joy, which is likely why it is consumed regularly even today in some areas of the world. More commonly than any other method of use, its dried leaves are steeped to make a tea.

GREAT FOR: Euphoria

BRAHMI *(Bacopa monnieri)*

This herb has been used for countless years to relieve stress and stimulate energy. It is unique in its creation of a balanced mix of calming and energizing actions. When consumed in a tea, this herb gently boosts the levels of serotonin and dopamine, the neurotransmitters responsible for mood. It is also possible to consume this herb in capsules and supplements, as larger quantities and consistent use are often needed to experience the greatest benefits.

GREAT FOR: Mood lift, energy boost

GOTU KOLA *(Centella/Hydrocotyle asiatica)*

This herb that is related to the carrot has been used historically for many purposes. You can find it in capsules, tinctures, and tablets, and used in skin creams and body scrubs. This herb is thought of as a brain tonic, and it is shown to assist the brain in remarkable ways. It is known to shield the brain from toxins and mood swings and can actually assist in overall brain health by enhancing and stimulating the growth the different parts of neurons.

GREAT FOR: Mood lift

CALAMUS ROOT *(Acorus calamus)*

This incredibly versatile herb is known for its spicy and bitter taste. It is popular in perfumes, as it has an aromatic smell. Historically, it has been used to reduce fatigue and headaches. Its effects have been connected to the stomach, and it is used to treat nausea-based stomachaches. Specifically, it is believed to ease nausea that is produced in relation to feelings of nervousness or disease. If you are feeling sad or nervous and notice an upset stomach, chewing this root could produce a calming sensation and open the door to happiness. Chewing the calamus root is also believed to produce a calm mind and relieve symptoms of anxiety, like racing thoughts. However, note that it can easily be used in excess, which will produce vomiting and other undesirable symptoms. Start by chewing a small piece of this bark and wait thirty minutes to notice its effect.

GREAT FOR: Anxiety, clarity

ST. JOHN'S WORT *(Hypericum perforatum)*

St. John's wort is a happiness herb that is great for serenity. It is a natural antidepressant and is believed to produce more serotonin within the brain. Serotonin is considered the happiness neurotransmitter, as it plays a crucial role in regulating mood. It is most often taken in capsule supplements.

GREAT FOR: Depression, anxiety, irritability

PASSIONFLOWER *(Passiflora incarnata)*

This flower can be used to brew teas that assist in producing calmness. Passionflower is considered to be a natural anti-depressant and is most commonly used to treat anxiety and overactive minds. By calming the mind, you can access sensations of bliss and happiness that are not available to the restless or distracted mind. Happiness can be best cultivated in the present moment, where anxiety and depression cease to thrive.

GREAT FOR: Anxiety, relaxation

KAVA KAVA *(Piper methysticum)*

Kava kava has been used in history as a ceremonial tool and social aid. Traditionally, people would drink a tea infused with kava kava to allow for better conversation and happier experiences while in a ceremony or in group events. It produces a mild sedative and pain-relieving effect, which fosters sensations of happiness, sociability, and stress ease. It does not produce such a heavy effect that you would feel intoxicated, but it does allow for subtle, pleasant relaxation. It is recommended that a person who has never consumed kava kava start with roughly 14 ounces of the tea for their first time. It is unusual to note that this herb actually gets stronger the more often you use it, so this dose is only recommended for a first-time experience.

GREAT FOR: Mood lift, sociability, stress, relaxation

OAT STRAW *(Avena sativa)*

Oat straw has had various industrial and medicinal uses over the years. It is said to be a mild antidepressant and contains many vitamins and minerals. The presence of vitamins and minerals is important to consider in producing happiness. Your mood is regulated by your brain and body. Vitamins and minerals promote the absorption of nutrients, which is a vital component of regulating mood, hormones, and neurotransmitters like serotonin and dopamine. Oats have also been known to be very helpful for individuals withdrawing from different substances and who may be experiencing mood disturbances.

Oat straw tea is helpful for gently regulating hormones. It is a wonderful premenstrual syndrome remedy and is also useful during all parts of the female reproductive cycle. It's light and uplifting properties help with mood regulation.

You can also consume oats themselves by simply having a delicious bowl of oatmeal! They're also used in various spa treatments, including oat washes, oat compresses, and oat facial masks. To make an oat wash, create a powder from oat flakes and blend with oil. Rub the resulting paste into the skin. The treatment can allow oats to work their way into your body through your biggest organ: your skin! Treating yourself to this spa experience is also bound to increase your sensations of happiness and relaxation.

GREAT FOR: Mood lift, depression, withdrawal

Joyful Journey Bath

Whether it's a fleeting moment or an ongoing battle, depression and hopelessness project a dark cloud above your head. It is hard to appreciate relationships, possessions, good fortune, and stability when situations seem drenched in negativity. The concept of self-care relates to small rituals that can restore feelings of well-being that you may have neglected when dealing with life's tribulations.

Taking a bath is relaxing and brings down a jumpy heart rate. Adding the ingredients for cleansing yourself spiritually, like herbal tea, healing crystals, and aromatherapy, creates the conditions necessary for a profound transformation. If you look within yourself to find motivation and express it to yourself on paper while doing this healing activity, you will come away from this joyfulness bath energized, grateful, and ready to tackle personal hurdles.

Gather the following materials:

* Paper
* Pen or pencil
* One or more pieces each of amber, clear quartz, moldavite, celestite, and rhodochrosite
* Lemon essential oil

* Ylang-ylang essential oil
* Two orange scented candles
* Fenugreek tea
* Organic honey
* Dried calendula

Prepare a cup or pot of fenugreek tea, which is sold in health food stores alongside fennel tea as an herbal remedy for breastfeeding mothers who want to stimulate milk production. Brew the tea before you get ready to fill up the bath and steep the leaves until the water becomes green. As you sip the tea, fully savor its tangy licorice tones and unique aftertaste. You should feel comfort from the warmth of the mug and mindfully process every sensation as the tea passes through your body. For sweetener, add a spoonful of organic honey.

Fenugreek tea aids digestion, alleviates constipation, and reduces bloating, and it has anti-inflammatory properties that benefit people who aren't currently nursing. Drinking a few cups over several days will act as a cleanse for the liver and the lymphatic system. If you have a cold, drinking fenugreek tea can help break up mucus in the respiratory system and give relief from the common cold. It also acts to prevent upper respiratory infections in those who suffer from hay fever and allergies. Finally, the potent seeds are praised for improving the growth and appearance of hair.

Since it's sold in the maternity isle, expect the tea to target the mammary glands in women. In India, fenugreek is called methi and is used as a spice in cooking; mothers are encouraged to eat plenty of fenugreek across North

Africa and the Middle East right after giving birth. Studies and long-held tradition demonstrate that fenugreek boosts lactation hormones, which also stimulate breast growth over time.

With this knowledge in mind, begin shutting off your devices so that no one may disturb you during your ritual, interrupting your positive energy with distressing news or messages. Put your phone in a different room entirely and adjust the lighting around your bathing area. Think about the balance between suffering and enjoyment in your life, and cast aside the negative parts of your day thus far. Create a space around you where you feel safety and gratitude for your tea and the wonderful bath you're soon to experience.

Start running the bath. Write down on a piece of paper a mantra or prayer that uplifts you. It can be as simple as "May this bath bring me joy," "May I be free from sorrow today," "I am strong enough to feel joy," or any combination of words that will bring you upliftment. Say the phrase out loud as you write it down. Place the paper with the words on it near your bath, within your line of sight. You may want to tape this paper to a wall so that it is safe from water or fire. Recite this mantra as you ignite each candle.

Place several drops each of ylang-ylang oil and lemon oil in your bath. Take a deep breath in and inhale these scents, mindfully noticing their differences and the aroma they create along with the orange candles in your bathroom. Both essential oils are mood boosters and exude joy with their noticeable fragrance. Your surroundings should begin to smell similar to a luxury spa.

Scatter leaves of dried calendula over the bathtub. Also known as pot marigold, the flowers of this plant are edible. Concentrated amounts of calendula have healing properties. The yellow flowers have a sunny effect on a ritual bath and are said to ward off negative energy. Calendula had sacred significance in Mayan and Aztec culture and continues to be used in Mexico during Día de Los Muertos ceremonies. In your bath, ask spirits for admiration, respect, and overall protection.

When the water is ready, gather your crystals and step into the bath.

Whether your amber stone has a fossilized bug inside or it's a honey-colored rock, this valuable crystal will make you feel more at ease with its ancient energy. Think of it as a little life-preserving talisman to bring you courage and make your deepest fears subside. Let it clear your mind and ease any stress you brought with you as you hold the piece of amber near your solar plexus to gain wisdom and power.

Holding a piece of clear quartz will direct the universe's energy into your body, especially if you hold the hexagonal piece toward you like an arrow. You'll feel more grounded and motivated to take on the future, and feelings of hopelessness or confusion will melt away. Appreciate the weight of your quartz piece; since clear quartz is relatively inexpensive, opt for a piece that is substantial and exudes strength. If you have a specific pain or ache somewhere, wave the quartz over the afflicted area, as its healing properties are said to sometimes provide medically significant relief from discomfort. Clear quartz is most in tune with the crown chakra, so move the crystal over your head to maximize your positive connection to the universe at large.

Moldavite is a highly powerful and costly crystal with effects so profound that dizziness and tingling in the hands are common while using it. Its mystical properties include a very high vibration and intense frequency, creating the conditions necessary for a transformative experience. The jade-green crystal links to the heart chakra and opens it to compassion and empathy toward others. When you engage with the moldavite, keep your intentions laser-focused, reflect on your mantra, and remind yourself of your agency to feel joy in this moment and moments to come. If you can't get your hands on a piece of precious moldavite, consider substituting moldavite bath salts, lotion, or another infused product for this ritual.

Light blue celestite is rumored to have divine, angelic energy and is conducive to spiritual transformations that result in feelings of selflessness and generosity. You will think more earnestly than you did before about your relationship to other people, and after the bath is over, your positive aura will have an impact on your social interactions. The desire to argue or be uncooperative in tricky situations evaporates as you wish to accept, rather than fight, poor circumstances. Feel the joy in knowing that compromise will come more easily in the future, after the bath has concluded. To absorb the energy and receive best results, hold the celestite near your forehead (the third eye chakra).

The last of your crystals is the rhodochrosite, a vibrant pink crystal associated with the heart chakra. Mindfully feeling this rock will produce a sense of wholeness and understanding, as though you are playing the role of a parent to yourself and telling yourself that things will be okay. It will propel you forward and give you excitement about future endeavors. Rhodochrosite heals trauma and stimulates courage to overcome one's obstacles. With the knowledge that satisfaction is yet to come, let that certainty fill you with hope and joy.

While admiring the shape, weight, color, and density of each crystal, deeply inhale and exhale in slow succession. Feel the glow of the candles near you and note the presence of the calendula flowers and essential oils. Wash your body with soap and repeat your mantra as needed, reaffirming your worth in the present moment.

When you are ready, emerge from the tub and wrap yourself in a clean towel. Once the tub is drained, the calendula will be left in the empty tub basin; it will not clog the drain, but the leaves will need to be removed. Don't worry about washing your hair during this ritual bath, as the purpose was to become joyful, not to shampoo and condition your hair. Take a shower at a later time to wash stray calendula leaves out of your hair, if need be. You should smell good from the essential oils having soaked into your skin during your bath.

Rapturous Ritual

Joy is the highest vibration in the known universe. It can heal your body. Your body is an amazing self-regulating, self-correcting wonder. After over fifteen years as a medical intuitive this truth is more resonant than ever. I have seen it with people throughout my career: joy heals. So, let's enact a joyful ritual to elevate your being.

You have the opportunity to rewrite patterns that are not aligned with the reality you choose to attract and create. This can be done in a way that permeates through your complete existence.

Your feelings and thoughts directly create your reality. You are a magnet. The principles of electromagnetics can be adapted to explain your existence perfectly. Electromagnetic energy deals in the currency of emotions and feelings. Any emotions or feelings you are experiencing will attract more of the same.

The energetic charge that is strongest in your electromagnetic field, also known as your aura or light body, is constantly attracting more of itself. Emotions and feelings are one of the greatest gifts of the human race, brought to us by the amazing chemicals of happiness and reward. We all possess an incredible capacity to experience emotion, and this is one of our most profound tools for learning.

People are particularly predisposed to master the mechanics of emotional electromagnetics. You are wired to transcend via your emotions. You are wired to attract selected electromagnetic energies of your choice by harnessing the power of your emotions.

Energy and matter dance together to create reality. Your way into this dance is through your capacity to consciously regulate and harness your emotions. Positive feelings vibrate quickly and healthily. Joy is the feeling in our repertoire with the highest vibration. Attracting joy is literally going straight to the source. It is the highest vibrational energy. Each ecstatic explosion of energy that created the universe was born of joy. To feel joy is to know infinity.

To start the ritual, ask yourself the following questions. You may answer them in your journal:

* What makes you feel good?
* What makes you feel good about yourself?
* What evokes joy for you?

Step 1

A dull feeling around your living space can seriously dampen the joy you're supposed to get from simply being at home. This might come in the form of dreary decorating or apathy toward tidying up. When you wake up in the morning, your surroundings ought to bring you hope and enthusiasm for the day ahead. Altering décor to achieve a more positive energy can be as simple as buying flowers or mixing an all-natural room spray with water and uplifting essential oils. Small changes can make huge differences in your psyche if they are intentional and symbolic.

Generally, the color yellow signifies joy and happiness, and in nature appears more vibrant than on paper: after all, the sun feeds all things that grow on planet Earth. Some days, we're discouraged because we can't see the sun at all in overcast, cloudy, or rainy skies. To combat this gloominess indoors, buy or pick a beautiful bunch of daffodils or marigolds as a present to yourself and your home. Daffodils in particular are associated with springtime, new beginnings, longevity, bliss, and positivity. Marigolds have been used in religious ceremonies all over the world for centuries as sacrificial flowers and are said to promote love and encouragement for another's growth. Add some beautiful, vibrant looking flowers to your environment to enliven it.

Step 2

Learn to be present to joy. Rub a bit of lemon essential oil on the insides of your wrists. Smell the invigorating scent. Now, repeat the following affirmation: "I am present in my body, and I am filled with pleasure and bliss."

How can you feel truly present? This question is asked by people from all walks of life, of every age, in all kinds of ways, like "How can I feel more alive?"

Start simple. With the palms of your hands, start at the soles of your feet and rub briskly, moving up your legs and body, and repeat aloud or in your mind, "I am here now. I am present." And just feel what it is like to be fully in your body. Really bring your awareness to that experience.

Now try to bring your conscious awareness to your feet, and really inhabit them. Then do this with your feet and

human bodies rotate and move more when stimulated by music that brings happy feelings. Watch yourself in a mirror if it enhances the experience and makes you feel sexy and cool. Open your voice and sing along. Singing moves energy in a major way; it is tremendously healing. Your enjoyment of the music you're dancing to will be magnified by this heightened sense of vibration in your body.

Step 6

In yoga, poses that work the abdominal core relieve emotional tension related to self-worth and well-being that inhibit our experience of joy. If you're feeling stressed out, upset, or overwhelmed and want to briefly center yourself, bust out a mat and breathe deeply through the two following poses.

Boat pose is best described as your torso and your legs forming a 45-degree angle. Get into this position by first sitting with your legs bent and your feet flat on the yoga mat, grounding your butt on the mat. Lean back a bit and lift your feet off the mat until your shins are parallel to the ground. Keep your spine and torso straight, so that your abs are lengthened and engaged. Have your arms sticking out straight ahead the same width as your shoulders, and after steady breaths and a few counts, straighten your legs at 45 degrees. Your arms should still be engaged, your lower back should be raised off the ground, and from the side, your body should look like an upright *V.* Hold this position for several full in-breaths and out-breaths. Relax your muscles and lie back. If done correctly, this pose tones hamstrings, back muscles, and upper thighs along with the abdominal core.

Next, try the bow pose. Lie down on your stomach, hands resting naturally at your sides. Breathe in, breathe out, and, keeping your knees at hip width, bend the knees until your heels nearly touch your butt. Grab the outer part of your ankles, hold them, and lift your thighs off your mat, drawing the rest of your body to the ceiling. Focus on planting your tailbone into the mat and lifting your heels, thighs, chest, and shoulders off the ground. As you lift your chest into the air, dig those shoulder blades into your upper back and hold that position for 15 to 30 seconds. Disengage the chest and thighs first, slowly lowering yourself down to the mat. When your head comes down to the mat, rest on your right ear. Do the bow pose several more times, alternating which side of the head meets the mat. A proper bow pose should target posture, open up the chest and lung area, and improve balance.

You can also modify this pose by using a yoga strap if you are not able to hold your ankles. Or do the half bow pose. To do this pose, lie flat on your stomach and place your chin gently on the mat. Extend both arms in front of you. Bend your right knee and reach your right arm back to gently take hold of your ankle. Lift your right heel toward the ceiling, thereby raising your torso and arm. You can rest your left hand on the mat or raise it in front of you. Hold the pose for a few seconds and then repeat it on the left side.

Now you can go forth all jazzed up with joy.

TURN HEARTBREAK TO LOVE

QUESTION 1

My idea of romance is:

1. Being with my partner.
2. My date giving me a nice foot rub.
3. My partner doing the dishes, so I don't have to.
4. Romance is dead.

QUESTION 2

Getting ready for a romantic date, I:

1. Go all out—sexy attire, mood lighting, etc.
2. Go to the salon.
3. Dress up a bit.
4. What date?

QUESTION 3

Without these components, romance is out:

1. I don't need props, just my partner.
2. Slow dancing with my partner.
3. The setting has to be just right. Music, candlelight, etc.
4. Wine, lots of it.

Add up the numbers of each answer you chose to get your score. For example, if you chose answer 4 for question 1, you will have 4 points for that question.

If Your Score Is 10 to 12

Oh dear. It sounds as though your love life could use a serious reboot. It could be that the main problem is that you are lacking time—you probably have a million things to do that seem more important, and you have a stressful life. Well, make some time—sex (solo or with a partner) is a great way to work off the stresses of the day.

* **Cinnamon oil:** This is an oil that helps to improve sexual desire and that will also assist you in recovering from stress and debilitating illnesses. A word of warning: cinnamon can be irritating to the skin, so if you are using it on your body, use a very highly diluted form.

* **Sweet orange oil:** While not strictly an aphrodisiac oil, this can help you to regain your sunny disposition and quell worries you might have. It works extremely well with cinnamon oil.

If Your Score Is 7 to 9

It's not like you never experience pleasure and romance, but you are also not setting the sheets on fire anytime soon, either. Here's how you can inject a bit more passion. When you ignite your desire, you heat up the meridians of the body via the kidneys. As the kidney channel builds energy, your lung meridian is warmed and activated, and any grief you are holding is able to be released. The lungs are notorious for storing emotional energy of grief.

* **2 drops of jasmine oil:** Jasmine is a potent aphrodisiac oil that has the added benefit of giving you a feeling of euphoria. It does not get much better than this. In Chinese medicine, jasmine builds kidney yang energy, which is responsible for libido and potency. A healthy libido is incredibly healing, and when you love and respect yourself, it can be an open door to deep experiences of unconditional love. You can mix jasmine oil with a carrier and massage a few drops on your back over your kidneys to really activate their self-healing and yang properties.

* **2 drops of ylang-ylang oil:** This oil has strong aphrodisiac properties and can help you to relax as well. The other benefit is that it is an easy scent to identify, so the minute you smell it, you know that passion could be around the corner.

If Your Score Is 5 or 6

You are feeling love and passion and experiencing pleasure, but you would benefit from even more. Use this blend.

* **2 drops of patchouli oil:** The eternal scent of the sixties flower child, patchouli oil stokes sexual desire and helps you relax at the same time.

* **2 drops of clary sage:** Clary sage has a balancing effect on the emotions, is good for treating depression, and also acts as an aphrodisiac. When placed in a carrier oil over the center of the chest it brings vital

chi, or energy, to the pericardium meridian, which can activate the energies of the heart.

If Your Score Is 3 or 4

Okay, so romance is alive and kicking for you. Want to add an extra level of excitement, passion, or tenderness?

* ✳ **2 drops of black pepper oil:** This will help give you the ardor to make love all night.
* ✳ **2 drops of rose oil:** Rose is the ultimate heart opener. It is the oil of unconditional love. Use to open to ecstasy and experiences of transcendent love.

All the Oils You Should Consider for Love and Romance

* ✳ **For lack of sexual desire:** cinnamon and sweet orange oil.
* ✳ **For frigidity or performance anxiety:** jasmine and ylang-ylang oil.
* ✳ **To start to lift off sexually:** patchouli and clary sage oil.
* ✳ **To spice things up:** black pepper and rose oil.

The oils listed previously are perfect to ignite your passion and open your heart to love. Sometimes, healing heartbreak is all about loving yourself and opening your heart to love in all of its forms. Imagine feeling passion and not having it be exclusively dependent on being in a couple. What if your love for yourself fanned the flame of pleasure and fed your inner passion, and a wonderful partner was just the icing on the cake?

There is nothing quite as romantic as getting a massage from your partner, so definitely put that on your to-do list and increase the wow factor by using the recipe provided below. There is just one caveat here – if you are using a massage oil and then will be using condoms, make sure that the oil is cleaned off properly before applying a condom. Condoms can break by exposure to oil-based substances. (That's why sexual lubricants are always water- or silicone based.)

Not all the oils on the list are going to work for you, and that is perfectly fine. Choose oils that you enjoy the scent of and that you can see yourself using over and over again. You can experiment with all of them, or just choose one or two—it's all up to you and what suits your taste and lifestyle.

Here are some recipes to try.

Passionate Perfume

1 cup sweet almond oil

5 drops rose oil

10 drops jasmine oil

Mix well in a glass or roll-on container. Shake before each application. Apply a little to your neck and to each wrist as you would with a traditional perfume.

Carpet Romance Scent

Granted, this one sounds a little weird, but hear me out: environment is especially important, so scenting the carpets in your home can enhance your pleasure and experience of self-love and passion.

1 cup baking soda

10 drops jasmine oil

10 drops ylang-ylang or cinnamon oil

Mix the ingredients in a sealed container and store overnight so that the scents can develop. Sprinkle over the bedroom carpet and leave in place for at least 2 to 3 hours before vacuuming it up.

Room and Linen Spray

1 cup distilled water

2 tablespoons witch hazel or vodka (helps the oils to disperse in the water)

10 drops cinnamon oil

10 drops sweet orange oil

Mix all ingredients in a spray bottle and spritz in the room as needed. Spraying the lampshades or curtains helps ensure that the scent lasts most of the day.

Essential oils can really help you rev up your romantic life—why settle for the same old boring routine when you can inject new life and passion quickly and easily?

Crystals for Unconditional Love and Romance

Is your love life a little stale or in need of some TLC? Is it nonexistent, or do you just want to liven things up a little and reignite the passion again? Or is your self-love and compassion in need of a reboot? Crystals can help you do that.

Rose Quartz

Every home should have at least one piece of rose quartz in it. It is a peaceful and gentle crystal that is also one of the best when it comes to attracting unconditional love into your life. It helps improve relationships with others and with yourself as well. It's a heart-opening stone. It pairs wonderfully with rose essential oil.

Always keep two pieces of this stone in your bedroom. Just before placing them, set an intention for finding true love and a healthy, respectful relationship and also set a clear intention to treat yourself with the utmost care and compassion. Pick up the stones and refresh your intentions as often as you'd like. This stone is powerful enough that you do not need to keep it on you.

It is also a good stone to use for your pets when they have separation anxiety or are feeling generally anxious. Tie a rose quartz stone to their collar to help calm them and soothe their nerves.

Rhodonite

This stone is useful if you need balance in your love life. Have you been feeling needy or lonely? Honor the truth of your emotions. How do you really feel? Accept yourself in your vulnerability and your victory. The totality of who you are is perfect and beautiful. Accept yourself exactly as you are. Rhodonite makes you feel nurtured and supported. It helps to dispel angst and jealousy so that you can start attracting love into your life and better cultivate self-love.

Garnet

Garnet is a fiery stone and perfect for reinjecting passion into your love life. It is very powerful and can heighten sexual attraction. It can help you feel more confident, which makes you more attractive. Look for a garnet that is deep red for the best results.

Jade

This is the stone to choose if your partner has broken your trust and you are choosing to work together to repair it. It helps to heal relationships and past hurts, and it can help you regain that initial spark. It is also a good stone to have in the early stages of a relationship because it encourages you to trust in love. It is a very lucky stone to wear.

Condition	Stone	Best Way to Use	Charge With
Attracting unconditional love	Rose quartz	In your environment	Moonlight/sun/ smudge/sand
Dispelling loneliness	Rhodonite	Carry it with you	Moonlight/sun/ smudge
Needing more passion	Garnet	Wear it as jewelry	Moonlight/sun/ smudge
Rebuilding trust	Jade	Keep it with you	Moonlight/sun/ smudge
Solving commitment issues	Emerald	Keep it with you	Moonlight/sun/ smudge

Emerald

Emerald is a good stone to access when there is a trouble with commitment—either from your side or your partner's side. Emerald helps to rebuild the friendship in the relationship, helping it move to a deeper level.

Love and Romance Plants and Flowers

To open yourself to love and romance, it is very important that the body be in a state of balance and ease. It is not possible to be completely present and sexually invigorated in the presence of anxiety, fear, and stress. The body is better able to prepare for romance when it is in a state of relaxation and balance. In fact, stress actually has adverse effects on the production of the chemicals of love. Many of these herbs allow us to open ourselves to love and energize us by encouraging the production of the same chemicals that we naturally produce when we are falling in love.

ROSE *(Rosa)*

Roses are the flowers most widely associated with love and romance. They have arguably become a commercialized symbol love, but believe it or not there is an explanation behind their romantic notoriety. Rose petals are said to open the heart. Certain species of roses are said to produce an aphrodisiac action. The cabbage rose is the species that is most often processed to produce many common products. It is this type of rose that is also known for its aphrodisiac qualities. Roses can be used for this purpose by simply growing them or arranging them within an indoor or outdoor space. It is true that giving roses on a special day to a loved one can allow for your love to deepen. Rose petals can also be used for aromatherapy by creating sachets. They can also be diffused to make teas or steams.

GREAT FOR: Heart opener, aphrodisiac

DAMIANA *(Turnera diffusa)*

The leaves of the damiana herb have been used traditionally as an aphrodisiac, because it is a stimulant and also increases levels of testosterone. Due to its testosterone-enhancing nature, this herb has been used successfully to treat men who have concerns such as premature ejaculation or impotence. However, this herb can be useful for women, too. Higher levels of testosterone can enhance a woman's libido. This herb also acts as a restorative medicine to the reproductive organs of both sexes. The dried leaves can be effectively consumed through a tea infusion. It is also sold in capsules.

GREAT FOR: Aphrodisiac, libido

ARJUNA *(Arjuna myrobalans/Terminalia arjuna)*

This herb is recognized for its capacity to strengthen the heart, not only physically but emotionally. The bark from the plant contains arjunetin, which is believed to have powerful medicinal properties. It is used to treat high blood pressure, heart failure, and other heart disease. While arjuna is known to strengthen the physical heart, its powerful effect is believed to benefit the emotional and energetic heart, too. Therefore, it is useful to ingest this herb when you are feeling heartbroken or disheartened. It is great medicine to use when you feel cold toward yourself or others or as if your heart is closed off. The bark can be ground into a powder. Put 1 tablespoon into 2 cups of water, and then boil down the mixture so that it reduces down to half the amount. Consume the mixture while it is still hot. Arjuna is also consumed in extract form or in capsules found in health food stores.

GREAT FOR: Heartbreak, heart opener

GOTU KOLA *(Centella/Hydrocotyle asiatica)*

This versatile herb is known for its many uses. Gotu kola is ingested in teas, capsules, tinctures, or tablets, and used in skin creams and body scrubs. Skin patches are also created from dried plant powder to treat skin conditions. It has also been taken to treat fertility issues. The leaves of this herb can be chewed or infused into a tea.

GREAT FOR: Fertility

CALAMUS ROOT *(Acorus calamus)*

Different groups and civilizations throughout history have found that chewing alamus root can to assist in sexual potency, produce motivation, and induce relaxation to aid in sexual rituals. It is thought to increase libido and acts as a sexual stimulant by transmuting dormant energy within the body into active sexual energy. If you are seeking to enhance your sexual desire, chewing a small piece of this bark is a great natural alternative to synthetic pharmaceutical options.

GREAT FOR: Libido, aphrodisiac, fertility

GOLDEN ROOT/ROSEROOT/ARCTIC ROOT/ RHODIOLA *(Rhodiola rosea)*

This herb is known to produce a positive mood, longevity, and an increased sex drive. It allows for an improvement in mental clarity, endurance, and mood. To enhance sex life, it is commonly taken in supplement form. Not only does this herb reduce stress and fatigue, which allows for a boosted sex drive, but it also is believed to increase levels of testosterone. In fact, any herb that reduces stress can be beneficial to increasing levels of testosterone, as the stress hormone cortisol is linked to lower levels of testosterone. Higher levels will naturally increase the libido. For men, this can result in more powerful and longer-lasting erections. It has also been linked to preventing premature ejaculation. For women, more testosterone equals more libido and more powerful orgasms as well as more energy and muscle tone. Testosterone is the ultimate antioxidant and one of the body's own fountains of youth. It can have a positive impact on both partners' sexual satisfaction. Rhodiola is a great natural supplement to use if you are looking to bring life back into your sexual relationship with a partner or with yourself.

GREAT FOR: Aphrodisiac, libido, sexual performance

GINSENG *(Panax ginseng/Panax quinquefolium/Panax notoginseng/Eleutherococcus senticosus)*

Ginseng is an herb that has many different species with various components and uses. It is usually consumed in a tea. The most common type of ginseng used to affect the mental and emotional state is Siberian ginseng (*Eleutherococcus senticosus).* Very high doses of any type of ginseng can produce adverse effects like nausea and insomnia. American and Asian ginsengs are known to produce estrogenic effects. Ginseng is great for women to increase their levels of estrogen. It should be avoided by men, especially men over fifty, as their levels of testosterone are already beginning to decline naturally. Ginseng produces an aphrodisiac effect when used. It contains steroidal glycosides, which have been established to be similar to human sex hormones. This may explain its aphrodisiac effects. Like many other herbs, it is considered to be an adaptogen, which simply means that it has body-balancing properties. When trying to increase libido or balance sexual drive, balancing the entire body and its hormones is always the prime and most important step.

GREAT FOR: Aphrodisiac, estrogenic, libido

CACAO *(Theobroma cacao)*

Cacao is the bean that is used to make chocolate. Cacao can be translated from Latin into "food of the gods," and for good reason. Much like roses, chocolate has become associated with love. This is for many logical reasons, as chocolate, or cacao in its more pure form, is an incredible tool for enhancing your experience of love. This is because it impacts the neurochemicals in the brain and body that are responsible for love and pleasure. Phenylethylamines (PEAs) are a class of chemicals that are produced naturally by the body when we notice that we are falling in love. PEAs are found in abundant amounts within cacao. Anandamide is another chemical to consider. It is produced when you exercise, and has been found in only one plant. You guessed it: cacao! It also contains certain enzymes that prevent the breakdown of anandamide, which allows us to hold on to that good post-workout feeling for even longer. Another component of cacao is the amino acid called tryptophan. This is a nutrient that is known to be incredibly mood enhancing. There has been some skepticism about the aphrodisiac properties of cacao in the past, but research is quickly revealing that the ancient practice of using cacao as an aphrodisiac has extensive scientific merit. Studies have also found that eating chocolate will increase levels of dopamine in the brain, which can not only help you get into the mood to make love, but also experience increased levels of pleasure. As with any herb that assists in love and romance, cacao uses its abundant nutritional value to help in preparing the body and mind for making love by fostering health in the entire body and mind. When consuming cacao, it is important to remember that a purer recipe is more effective! Chocolate that is made with much sugar and milk will produce little to none of the above-mentioned medicinal effects. Dark chocolate of the highest concentration that is organic and minimally sweetened is the best choice.

GREAT FOR: Aphrodisiac, mood lift, pleasure enhancer, euphoria

No More Loneliness and Aphrodisiac Bath

Humans need to feel loved. Sometimes we feel pain because we don't have a partner and everyone around us seems to have someone special. Other times, we're sure about our feelings for someone who intimidates us or with whom we're afraid to express intimacy. It's also hard to be in love with someone miles away, or with someone who does not feel mutual lust. Partnership is tricky, and loneliness aches. If clichés about desirability are true, we must care for ourselves before expecting a feeling of worthiness to come from another person. Preparing a steamy bath for yourself is a lot like gifting yourself a romantic date.

Using the divine power of precious crystals and herbs, this bath ritual will unclog your heart chakra and break down barriers built up from trauma. Like cholesterol in the arteries, an unhealthy heart chakra has psychological issues slowing it down: sadness, loneliness, long-held grudges, betrayal. You might feel anxious, unwanted, ashamed, or resentful over physical or emotional intimacy and not know how to address those feelings. The smell of rose and the influence of assorted rocks represent gateways to the heart chakra, located energetically in the chest area. Traditionally, pink and green correspond to the heart chakra, which is why you will light pink candles, drink green tea, and center yourself with two pieces each of pink and green gems.

Gather the following materials:

* Paper
* Pen or pencil
* One or more pieces each of rose quartz, jade, green aventurine, and pink tourmaline
* Rose otto essential oil
* Jasmine essential oil
* Four pink candles
* Rose-scented soap
* Decaf jasmine green tea
* Dried hawthorn berry

Of the wide selection of green teas on the market, jasmine is one of the most delicate and flowery variants. In a French press or pot of boiling water, combine teabags or loose-leaf jasmine green tea with dried hawthorn berry, found in health food stores. Hawthorn berry is used in infusions and teas for an aphrodisiac effect. Strain the tea when the color becomes noticeably green (around 5 minutes). As you sip the brew, focus on mindfully consuming your beverage, making sure you do not let the tea disappear without actively appreciating its taste and the warm feeling on your hands.

With mindfulness as a priority in this ritual, power down your devices. Whether you've been talking all day to an exasperated lover or you've been isolated for weeks, take the time to withdraw into a cocoon of soothing scents and sensations. Dim the lights. Think about the connection your mind has to your body and immerse yourself in the present moment.

Start running the bath. Undress and wrap yourself in a robe. Take out the pen and paper and, taking a deep breath, prepare to become emotionally exposed and vulnerable. You are safe.

Write down on a piece of paper a mantra, affirmation, or prayer that gives you hope, such as "I am beautiful," "I am sexy," or "My heart is open and I enjoy pleasure daily."

For inspiration, dwell on this bit of wisdom from Buddhist monk Thich Nhat Hanh:

> *Words can travel thousands of miles.*
> *May my words create mutual understanding and love.*
> *May they be as beautiful as gems,*
> *as lovely as flowers.*

Or these lines from the poet Rumi:

> *This is what I see.*
> *The world is green,*
> *And everywhere there is a garden.*
> *I see your face,*
> *luminous like a rose.*
> *I see you happy,*
> *you are laughing.*
> *Everywhere there is a gem,*
> *inflamed from the Beloved's mine.*
> *Everywhere there is a soul,*
> *connected to another soul.*

You want to hope and pray that your desires bring no harm to anyone, so that they may earnestly be fulfilled.

Simply ask that all your intentions be for the highest good of all life and in accordance with universal natural law: helping all and harming none.

It's your right to feel good and to obtain freedom through expressing your sexuality. Become aware of your natural body vibration and energy level, and claim your body as an extension of your spiritual self. Think about your chest as the gateway to finding pleasure of all kinds. According to the theory of these metaphysical energy centers, the heart is the true middle of your body, the "electromagnetic bridge where sex and the soul meet" (Raether). If this chakra is unbalanced, we can be led astray by poor decision making. In a way, satisfying your sexual needs satisfies the heart's nagging wants, which is the only hope you have of achieving metaphysical alignment along your spine. This is as simple as just loving yourself in your nakedness.

Place several drops each of rose otto oil and jasmine oil in your bath. If you have a diffuser for essential oil, add some drops and turn it on to add perfumed mist to the air. Enjoy the intoxicatingly sweet garden smell, taking deep breaths and long sips of tea while the bath fills to your liking.

Arrange the pink candles in a safe place, where they won't fall or burn the paper message. Hum or recite the mantra while igniting each wick. If possible, put the gems alongside the candles. Slowly dip your toes into the water and lower yourself until submerged in a sitting position in the bathtub. Begin washing yourself with some rose-scented soap to maximize the benefits of aromatherapy. When you're ready, settle comfortably and engage with the crystals.

Rose quartz is so strongly associated with love that retailers often sell the light pink crystal in the form of a polished heart. Its gentle energy magnifies the positive, rewarding aspects of love and makes doubts evaporate. This is especially true for all instances of unconditional love in your life, whether it's family, friends, or your partner there for you in any and all tough situations. Let your heart pulse against the jewel for a moment, imagining it as an amulet hanging on a string around your neck.

Rose quartz reinvigorates the spirit after trauma. If your pain is from a separation or the end of a relationship, the crystal will point you in the direction of light and optimism. Its properties fight loneliness and bring comfort when needed. Other figures in your orbit may come out of the woodwork and present themselves as dependable sources of support. This will bring you a cosmic sense of belonging in the universe.

Focus on your piece of green aventurine. If your heart is broken, take deep breaths with the crystal on your chest. Summon the great capability of the aventurine, which will help you take charge and make decisions. It is a transformer as well as a seeker crystal, so you can trust that incredible new experiences are on the horizon after this ritual bath. Not only will you encounter new opportunities, but your future self will also be better equipped to make the most of high-stakes situations. Allow the green aventurine to rebalance your heart chakra and soothe dark, existential thoughts.

If you are in a relationship, the green aventurine acts as a harmonizer, protecting the heart during periods of discord and putting your energy and your partner's in balance. Instead of fighting, you'll show compassion for one another. Ask the stone to bring you both emotional calm and infinite generosity.

Place jade on your breastbone to get a soothing, calming effect. Take more deep breaths and repeat your affirmation. Like the rose quartz, think of the jade as an amulet around your neck. Your thoughts should feel more stable as you relax every tense muscle. Emotional health is greatly affected by sleep, and close contact with jade is said to promote restfulness and meaningful dreams. To spread this intention to the brain, hold the jade on your forehead for at least ten seconds. Notice that this ritual leaves you in a serene mood for bedtime, ready to meet the next day.

Visualize a pink glow. Squint at the pink candles and picture a rosy aura surrounding you and your space. Imagine that the hue is entering your field of vision solely from the pink tourmaline. The warmth of the bath is larger than the bathtub and you, and it will linger on your body long after the water disappears down the drain. The pink tourmaline is emanating a fertile energy that draws people to you like gravity. Even after a short time, those you meet will take note of the kindness and love that you project outward, and they will want to get to know you. This will happen when your self-love proves genuine and hope is restored that you possess inherent worth in society. Sometimes, that is difficult after a breakup or during a lovers' quarrel. However, the pink tourmaline will push away those feelings of self-doubt. It is a nurturing, restorative stone.

Conclude your bath and wrap yourself in a towel or robe. Feel at ease in your unique skin, and don't lose sight of the oneness with your mind and body. The next conversation you have, be an active listener and be fair to your partner, friend, or family member. Have faith in your renewed spirit and zeal. You are confident, taking care of yourself and trying your best.

Embracing Love Ritual

As the saying goes, "Love is all around us." Make a commitment today to see and experience love *at least* once per hour. Try it for a day. Notice the way a co-worker holds the door for you with a smile. Notice the love between the couple in the car next you that kisses at the stoplight. Notice people connecting with each other. Notice caring in action all around. Put your focus on love and change your life. I dare you.

Look for the truth and authenticity in love. Judgments aren't truths. Feeling self-consciousness is not truth. Wanting to act and appear a certain way because of social decorum is not necessarily truth. These are all born of fear and insecurity. Fear is the opposite of love, and you can flip your fears on their head and turn them into love. Insecurity is being scared of your authentic self. It is the belief that your true, authentic self is not as magnificent as it actually is. Let go of that insecurity and do something totally gutsy and feel the relief in that. Share your true feelings. Express your love for family, friends, pets, and life.

Let life revive you spiritually and emotionally during this ritual. Sometimes people come into your life for just that reason. We meet those soul-connected people at the perfect times. Whether it's the friend you get together with, and your faith in the opposite gender is renewed because he is decent and kind or she is honest and caring, or the boss who believes in you and gives you a chance to leap into the big leagues because of your creativity, or even the loving dog that snuggles you and licks your face because she is so happy to see you every single time you come home.

We're emotional beings. When we embrace this, we can open to deeper experiences of love and connection and enhance our quality of life. Our connections and the love they are made of may even be part of why we are here. These connections might help us solve our existential crises and learn to be present to the amazing blessing of being here on Earth among billions of other souls as an interconnected web of love. In the end, we are all one.

Step 1

What better way to celebrate authentic love than to give it? Make a list today of five ways you can share your love with others today. The more you give, the more love flows back to you. The more you share, the more you reap. The more you choose to live love the better, more pleasurable life you will lead. Try it today.

Step 2

Be kind. First, to yourself. No negative self-talk, no admonishments for forgetting to send out cards, just kindness in everything you say to yourself. And be kind to others 100 percent of the time. Even when you are in the slowest line on the planet at the grocery store, practice serenity and be kind to the cashier instead of impatient and grouchy. It's pretty simple. Place your relentless focus on kindness.

Step 3

Open your heart to love. Have no expectations about dates and romance; just give yourself a pass. Simply open your heart to the love from your nieces, nephews, pets, friends, grandma, and spouse and focus continually on that love. Share your love. Say "I love you" to every family member and friend, deliver the words with a big hug, and watch people soften and tension ease before your eyes.

Step 4

Create and uphold at least two self-nurturing rituals on crucial days this week. Make a list in your journal so you are prepared to practice these, and choose at least one to do now. For example, create a delicious breakfast in bed. Get up in the morning and make waffles with berries and whipped cream and then bring the food back to bed on a pretty tray before checking your phone, turning on the TV, or otherwise engaging with the outside world. Enjoy a favorite movie for some comic relief while enjoying hot chocolate after giving yourself a peppermint oil foot massage. Or put a home spa day that is nonnegotiable on your schedule. You get the idea. You have the power to nurture yourself, care for yourself, and through that focus open your heart to real love.

Step 5

Meditate on the feeling and idea of love. Pour yourself a delicious cup of tea. You might like to try tulsi tea infused with rose or passionflower. Next, place a little rose essential oil on the center of your chest and smell the scent deeply.

Lie down in a comfortable position and practice deep abdominal breathing. In your mind repeat the mantra *Ahem prema*. It is a Sanskrit mantra meaning "I am Divine Love." Focus on the way this mantra feels in your body as you say it. Allow your consciousness to relax and your mind to unfocus as you continue repeating it for as long as you would like. You can place your hands on your chest with the energy of your heart during this meditation. When it feels complete, drink some more tea, recenter yourself, and go about your day.

Try out the supine heart-opening goddess pose to open your heart and connect yourself with your emotional essence. As you rest in the pose you can breathe deeply and repeat the mantra, "I am love." Place a drop of rose essential oil on your heart area and contemplate the endless nature of unconditional love.

Opening your heart to love can be scary. What if you get hurt? What if it doesn't last? What if you are rejected? What if you aren't loved back? But love is the ultimate power in the universe, and if you miss out on love, whether it is romantic, with friends or pets, or even for yourself, you are missing out on the richness of life. Choose to open your heart to love. Make it a conscious choice. Your heart is wise and capable beyond what your mind can do. Your mind is limited. Your heart is limitless. Place your bets on the heart.

If you want to have a more open heart try this:

* Bring your attention into the center of your chest.
* Feel the energy there. Envision it glowing.
* Let your heart energy radiate. Just feel it and notice if it pulses or feels warm. Your attention helps it to radiate.
* Ask your heart if it wants to open. Listen for its answer. You may feel it emotionally or physically or via your senses. Visualize your heart responding and opening.
* If it is apprehensive, ask it why.
* What fears come up?
* Breathe into them and open into love. Feel the breath go into the center of your chest. Breathe deeply and relax. Keep doing this breathing into your heart and simultaneously let yourself relax. Relaxing is opening.
* Now say aloud, "I choose to open my heart. I draw to me openhearted people for my highest good. I allow my life to be full of love."

TURN
FEAR
TO
FREEDOM

WE ALL FEEL FEARFUL SOMETIMES. It's not something that we talk about very much. It's not common or even a widely acceptable topic of conversation. At best, we share our deepest feelings with our closest friends or family or a trusted partner. Fear is a primal emotion. It's something that we are instinctively wired to feel in potentially dangerous situations. Babies are born with a startle reflex and a hardwired fear of darkness. These are nature's attempts at keeping us safe. As humans evolved, a startle reflex or an aversion to the dark in a baby or small child might be the difference between wandering out of the tribal dwelling into the dark night and getting lost or staying close to a parent and remaining safe.

As evolving, conscious beings, we have an opportunity to transform our fear, whether it is primal or emotional, to freedom. Freedom comes from a sense of empowerment. Sometimes it comes from confidence or courageousness. And sometimes it comes from radical self-love and self-acceptance. Oftentimes, when we allow ourselves to surrender to what is happening, how we feel, and the interconnection of all life, we are able to let go of fear in a way that is deeper and more profound then we've yet to experience.

In this section, we will explore all kinds of ways that you can turn fear into freedom. We will talk about essential oils that can help you tap into your own inner wellspring of confidence. We will share lovely, courage-filled rituals that you can prepare for yourself. We will explore which types of minerals and crystals can help you invoke a sense of self-worth. We will also explore different plants and flowers and ways that you can use them to promote surrender. Then, we will meditate together to cultivate freedom. Finally, we will indulge in an empowerment ritual together. Let's steep ourselves in emotional freedom.

Courageous Oils

Self-esteem can be a tricky thing for most people. You could be feeling really good about yourself only to have someone's offhand comment make you step back and feel chastened. Building up your self-esteem means coming to the realization that other people's opinions of you are none of your business. You must get to a point where you can easily handle the good and bad comments and take both in stride. Fear can be transformed into freedom when you can surrender to the beautiful truth of who you are. Within you there is an infinite reservoir of self-worth and integrity—tap into it and alchemize your consciousness.

Which oils will work the best for you? Answer a few quick questions and find out.

QUESTION 1

When I give my opinion, I:

1. Give it straight off the bat. I am entitled to my own opinion and am usually right.

2. Offer it in a well-reasoned way and consider what others think.

3. Will usually temper it a bit. I want others to like me.

4. Wait to hear what the others are saying. I don't really trust my own opinion.

QUESTION 2

When someone criticizes me, I:

1. Listen to what they say and get on with my life. Criticisms don't faze me.

2. Take in what they say and work out whether it is a fair comment or not.

3. Believe them and hope to do better.

4. Feel intense self-doubt.

QUESTION 3

When I see someone I would like to talk to, I:

1. Walk up to them and introduce myself.

2. Speak to someone I know about getting introduced to them.

3. Find out what I can about them from someone I know so I know what their interests are.

4. Don't bother. They won't find me interesting anyway.

Add up the numbers of each answer you chose to get your score. For example, if you chose answer 4 for question 1, you will have 4 points for that question.

If Your Score Is 10 to 12

Your self-esteem levels are low, and you are probably missing out on a lot of interesting things as a result. What you need is to shore up your courage and confidence. Practice positive affirmations like "I love and accept myself exactly as I am" or "I am proud of who I am and I allow myself to shine." Here are some oils to help you do just that.

* ✳ **2 drops of jasmine oil:** This is the perfect oil for restoring confidence in yourself. It will leave you feeling blissfully happy, so sniff it when you have to handle some criticism.
* ✳ **2 drops of geranium oil:** This oil helps to balance your moods, helps you to relax and feel less stressed, and enables you to better handle stress.

If Your Score Is 7 to 9

It's time to fortify yourself with self love and inner strength. You don't value your own worth highly enough, and it is time to stop this cycle.

* ✳ **2 drops of bergamot oil:** Bergamot oil has been nicknamed the sunshine oil because it helps you to feel happier and more confident.
* ✳ **2 drops of sandalwood oil:** Sandalwood oil is great for calming your nerves. It has a deep scent and can always be relied on when it comes to calming jitters.

If Your Score Is 5 or 6

You are relatively confident—you are not the life of the party, but you are also not a wallflower. All you need is a bit of help in building up your confidence even more.

* **2 drops of neroli oil:** Neroli can help you feel happier and more confident.
* **2 drops of clary sage:** Clary sage has a balancing effect on the emotions, is good for treating depression, and also acts as an aphrodisiac.

If Your Score Is 3 or 4

Confidence is not a problem for you, is it? You might benefit from oils that help with keeping you calm and promoting introspection.

* **2 drops of frankincense oil:** This will help you to focus during meditation and help you to become more mindful of your surroundings.
* **2 drops of vetiver oil:** This will help you feel centered and always on an even keel.

All the Oils You Should Consider for Self-Esteem

* **For lack of confidence and low self-esteem:** jasmine and geranium oil.
* **To boost your sense of your own worth:** bergamot and sandalwood oil.
* **To boost confidence a couple of notches:** neroli and clary sage oil.
* **To encourage introspection:** frankincense and vetiver oil.

Let's move on now and look at recipes that will help you to incorporate essential oils easily.

Confidence Spritzer

1 cup grapeseed oil

5 drops sandalwood oil

10 drops jasmine oil

5 drops neroli oil

Place everything into a clean atomizer and mix thoroughly. Spritz on your body or in the room whenever you need a boost.

Walking on Sunshine

This will perk up your carpet and allow you to enjoy the scent of your chosen oils throughout the day.

1 cup baking soda

10 drops cedarwood oil

10 drops geranium or vetiver oil

Mix the ingredients in a sealed container and store overnight so that the scents can develop. Sprinkle over the bedroom carpet and leave in place for at least two to three hours before vacuuming it up.

Night Cream of Dreams

This is perfect for someone who has dry, damaged skin. If you feel that it is too heavy, replace the macadamia nut oil with plain aqueous cream.

1 cup thick aqueous cream

¼ cup macadamia nut oil

¼ cup rosehip oil

5 drops sandalwood oil

10 drops geranium oil

5 drops jasmine oil

5 drops rose oil

Blend all the ingredients together and apply after your normal cleansing routine at night.

Empowered Day Dry Shampoo

This will soak up oil on your scalp and build volume in your hair. It will also shroud your strands in the scent of fragrant oils throughout the day.

1 cup of cornstarch

10 drops bergamot oil

10 drops jasmine oil

Mix together the ingredients in a sealed container and store overnight so that the scents can develop. Sprinkle onto the hair roots and then vigorously massage your scalp to disperse the powder. Use a damp cloth to clean off any powder that spills onto your face.

Essential oils are especially helpful for those with self-esteem issues. They help to address the issues directly and improve your mood. But their influence goes farther than that: they help to alleviate anxiety and stress so that you feel more able to take on the world.

Brave and Daring Crystals

Sometimes, we could all use a little boost of confidence or some courage. Crystals are an excellent way to imbue yourself with the kind of bravery and self-worth that you need.

Sunstone

Sunstone is an excellent crystal to use when your confidence needs a boost. The iridescence of the crystal reminds you that it is time to shine, and the crystal itself subtly boosts your energy levels and feeling of self-worth.

Citrine

Citrine has long been considered the success stone. It is a phenomenal stone to keep with you if you have a busy day ahead because it boosts your mood, energy levels, and confidence and can help ward off negative energy. If someone says something unkind to you, citrine will help you completely ignore it.

Golden Beryl

Another sunny stone, this one is good if you need a boost for an interview or if you are vying for a promotion. It is an excellent stone for leaders as it boosts your confidence in your decision-making abilities.

Condition	Stone	Best Way to Use	Charge With
Showing you at your best	Sunstone	In your environment where you can see it	Moonlight/sun/ smudge/sand
Best when you have a crisis of confidence	Citrine	Carry it with you	Moonlight/sun/ smudge
When you need confidence for an interview	Golden beryl	Wear it as jewelry	Moonlight/sun/ smudge
Blocking negativity	Hematite	Keep it with you or use as jewelry	Moonlight/sun/ smudge
Regaining courage after an emotional trauma	Moonstone	Keep it with you	Moonlight/sun/ smudge
Assertiveness and public speaking	Blue chalcedony	Wear it as a necklace or pendant	Moonlight/sun/ smudge

Hematite

Hematite has a very reassuring weight to it, and it is excellent for blocking negativity from others. If you feel that someone does not have your best interests at heart, a hematite necklace will help you block negative energy and boost your confidence. You will feel more able to cope. You can own your space and be strong within your being, and then the energy of others will not affect you. It will also help you keep your focus.

Moonstone

This is a crystal that is undeniably beautiful. Much like the moon, from which it takes its name, it exudes a gentle, calming energy. If you are fearful or are trying to overcome a phobia, this is the right stone for you. If you have recently been through an emotional situation, moonstone can help you to heal and restore your confidence.

Blue Chalcedony

This crystal is perfect if you need to give a speech in public or if you need to stand up for yourself. It has long been associated with the throat chakra and is effective if worn as a necklace or pendant that ends with a point. Blue chalcedony helps you to become assertive and thus more confident.

Bold and Fearless Plants

Confidence and courage are feelings that can be difficult to manifest if you find yourself often consumed by self-doubt, worry, stress, or symptoms of anxiety and depression. Therefore, some herbs and flowers that also help with stress will assist with cultivating confidence and courage. These herbs and flowers are great to consider using if you need to prepare for public speaking, make an important decision, or push yourself into action.

LEMON BALM *(Melissa officinalis)*

Lemon balm is an herb in the mint family. It is a very gentle herb that is so safe, it is frequently recommended for children. It is known to be used to combat feelings of nervousness and social anxiety. However, if you consume lemon balm when you are not in a nervous or anxious state, it can be used to cultivate confidence. You can consume the dried herb in a tea to produce a sense of courage and confidence. A good recommendation is to take around three cups of this tea a day to maintain this sense of confidence.

GREAT FOR: Confidence

VALERIAN *(Valeriana officinalis)*

This herb is used to calm yourself. Feeling calm is an incredibly vital component to cultivating confidence and releasing fear. When we are presented with social situations where we do not feel confident, we sometimes create a mental narrative that centers around low self-esteem and low self-worth. We may have a hard time letting go of feelings of fear, and that can keep us immobilized. Valerian can help reduce the anxiousness and thoughts associated with feeling fearful. When we are calm and our nervous system is not on high alert, we can perform at our best. This herb can be consumed in tea steeped for 15 minutes or taken in a concentrated extract form. The extracts can be found in capsules in any health food or supplement store.

GREAT FOR: Confidence, self-esteem

GINSENG *(Panax ginseng/Panax quinquefolium/Panax notoginseng/Eleutherococcus senticosus)*

Ginseng has many different species from different areas of the world. Its medicinal benefits overlap in many of these sections, because it is known to reduce stress, improve alertness, and focus the mind. This is an excellent tea to drink if you are planning for a situation that may require confidence and courage, as it helps to lower blood pressure and ease the mind. It is said to improve mood by fostering an overall sense of well-being. This is incredibly important when fostering confidence and courage. It is also commonly used in capsules as a supplement.

GREAT FOR: Confidence, stamina, alertness

PEPPERMINT *(Mentha balsamea Wild.)*

Peppermint is an herb that contains menthol. Menthol is known to produce a calming action on the nervous system, which is a vital component in fostering confidence and courage. When your mind is not preoccupied with feelings of doubt and worry, you can step into a relaxed and productive state. You can step into your true, confident self. Consuming mint tea is a great method for receiving the benefits of this herb. Using dried mint that you have grown or collected yourself is a lovely way to source this herb if you are able. By consuming mint regularly, you can increase your self-esteem and enhance your overall life outlook.

GREAT FOR: Alertness, focus, optimism, self-esteem

RED CLOVER *(Trifolium pratense)*

This herb is commonly known as the women's herb, likely because it can help with menstrual and menopausal symptoms. It can be consumed in supplemental capsules to access some of these benefits, but it can also easily be consumed in a tea. It helps your sense of self-esteem due to its ability to increase levels of serotonin. You may find better benefits if you purchase (or grow) the dried herb rather than using commercial tea bags, as they may be less potent or grown inorganically and contain contaminants. This herb is also known to increase levels of concentration, allowing you to confidently focus on the task at hand.

GREAT FOR: Focus, self-esteem

CACAO *(Theobroma cacao)*

The "food of the great goddesses" deserves recognition as a tool for confidence and courage. The translation from Latin is directly "food of the gods" but we will take a bit of poetic license here and expand it to food of the goddess as well. The cacao bean can be consumed in many ways, including raw, by chewing the bean or grinding it into food or drinks. Cacao produces many desirable effects and assists the body in overall health. If you are seeking a confidence or courage boost, consuming some cacao is a great idea. If you consume a cacao beverage, you are affecting the neurotransmitters, such as dopamine and serotonin, that allow you to feel happier and have fewer inhibitions. You can decrease your sense of fear and enhance your sense of courage. It also increases the chemical related to your adrenal system called phenylethylamine, which plays a role in increasing excitement. Often when you are nervous or lack confidence, you feel anxious. Cacao is a great tool to transmute feelings of anxiety into excitement. Excitement can be a powerful driving force to act courageously.

GREAT FOR: Alertness, mood lift, focus, heart opener

WHITE SANDALWOOD *(Santalum album)*

This herb is another one that is considered to be a brain tonic. White sandalwood is an evergreen tree and is very different from red sandalwood. It is used in food, as well as in fragrances and spa treatments. It is said to have properties that enhance concentration and allow you to focus. If you are looking to lift your mood, improve your self-esteem, and enhance your ability to concentrate, using white sandalwood as part of your spa routine may help you to achieve these goals. Sometimes sandalwood is burned for aromatherapy and cleansing spaces (smudging).

GREAT FOR: Calming, focus, mood lift, mental strength

CALAMUS ROOT (*Acorus calamus*)

Chewing calamus root can produce various desirable sensations. With any herb or medicine, your intention is a vital component. If your intention is to increase your feelings of confidence and courage, using this herb could be incredibly beneficial. It has been used traditionally to improve symptoms associated with anxiety. If you are feeling nervous or unsure of yourself, chewing a small piece of this root could help clear that doubtful energy and replace it with sensations of ease and calmness. This is especially useful in stressful situations requiring your confidence, as this root is known to help clear the mind at just such times. Additionally, it has been known to produce energy and motivation coming from this calm space. It can help to produce that extra push that you may need to take matters into your own confident and courageous hands.

GREAT FOR: Motivation, calming

GOLDEN ROOT/ROSEROOT/ARCTIC ROOT/ RHODIOLA (*Rhodiola rosea*)

This root is also believed to help us perform under stress. It is adaptogenic and great for long-term use. Rhodiola capsules are a wonderful herb to use to feel more fluidity in your life and have more emotional flexibility and strength to face life's challenges.

If you need to make a special presentation or are in some other situation that involves a higher level of pressure or stress but requires a certain level of confidence and courage, then this root can be a great herb to use. It is popularly sold in extract form in various herbal supplements that are typically available in health food and vitamin stores. There are also dietary supplement powders with golden root that can be added into things like smoothies and juices to access the medicinal benefits.

GREAT FOR: Confidence, de-stress

SHANKAPUSHPI *(Convolvulus pluricaulis)*

This powerful herb is said to reduce stress and anxiety and is considered adaptogenic, which means it helps to balance the overall body. It also boosts concentration and memory. This combination makes it a great herb to use to cultivate confidence. If you are experiencing restlessness, irritability, aggression, feelings of being overwhelmed or stressed, mental fatigue, or anger, this herb could be perfect for you. Using this herb has been found to affect the brain's hormones and neurotransmitters, including dopamine, positively. Dopamine regulates your mood and fosters an overall sense of well-being and confidence. Shankapushpi is often found in a powder, extract, or herbal paste form. The dosage depends on the form you are taking, but it is not a problem if you dose incorrectly because there are no known negative side-effects from using this herb.

GREAT FOR: Mood lift, confidence, de-stress, self-esteem

Taking a bath or touching a crystal won't lead to total liberation under real oppression, but in order to care for others, we must first care for ourselves. Bathing is a basic need, but it doesn't have to be a forgettable moment in your routine. Indulge in a ritual bath with crystals, homemade herbal tea, positive affirmations, candles, and aromatherapy to relieve any momentary psychic pressure.

The thing about caring for yourself is it increases your confidence. A result may be the courage to change any circumstances in your life that do not bring you joy or peace. *You* are sovereign over your life. No one else. If your heart's desires are not manifest, only you have the power to take action to change that. Let this confidence bath help you prepare to own your life and your space with valor.

Big or small, ruminating on the powers of crystals can boost courage and fight against misplaced fears. As your sense of smell is stimulated by pleasant smells and your taste buds savor a perhaps unfamiliar brewed beverage, you'll be even more receptive through your chakras to the age-old properties of rocks and minerals. You'll need a small amount of preparation, an open mind, and a minute to breathe, as well as a good crystal store. Let's get soaking!

Gather the following materials:

* Paper
* Pen or pencil
* One or more pieces each of smoky quartz, black (polished) obsidian, blue kyanite, and amethyst

* Lemongrass essential oil
* Passionflower essential oil
* Lemongrass bar soap
* One red candle
* One white candle
* Elderflower tea
* Dried astragalus

These ingredients may be uncommon to you, but they are highly beneficial. Elderflower fights inflammation, cold, fevers, and allergies, and stimulates relaxation. Dried astragalus root comes from a pea plant found in northeast Asia (it's known as *huang qi* in Chinese), and like ginseng, it's an adaptogen that helps the mind respond better to stress. Astragalus has similar anti-inflammatory and antiviral properties to those of elderflower and works to strengthen your immune system.

First, make a brew of elderflower tea mixed with dried astragalus in a pot of boiling water. Once the mixture steeps for enough that the herbs are fully soaked and the water is a rich color, strain the tea for serving. As you begin to fill your bathtub, take mindful sips of this elixir with the intention that these natural antioxidants will protect you from the setbacks of poor health. Freedom from disease can be achieved by balancing the root chakra, which will be a focal point of our ritual.

Meditate on the idea that you are worthy and perfect exactly as you are. Confidence and self-worth are your birthright because you are magnificent. Let these truths seep into your skin and bones. Feel your ancestors cheering you on from beyond the veil, channeling confidence and good luck in your direction. Accept it.

If you have an aromatherapy diffuser, add drops of lemongrass oil and passionflower to its chamber as well as some drops in your bath. As the sweet scent fills your bathroom, you'll feel an overall sense of calm and serenity. Lemongrass is sold in nearly every essential oil line and can be used as an anxiety-reducing sleep aid with a little dab of oil between the brows at bedtime. It can also be rubbed on hands to alleviate "texting thumb," and injury from repetitive use. Apply the oil to the affected area daily. Passionflower essential oil is harder to find but will produce a feeling of euphoria during your ritual, especially when paired with the soothing lemongrass.

Grab your journal and pen and write the following sentence while saying it out loud: "I am powerful, and I stand for my worth." Rip that page out of your journal and place it over the faucet or somewhere where you will be able to see it during your bath. That phrase is the keynote for your entire bath time.

Using your journal, begin brainstorming affirmations about letting go of stress, expectations, resentment, and false perceptions. They can be in the form of a mantra, a prayer, a wish, or an inspirational quote. For example, as a jumping-off point, here is a wise observation about suffering from Buddhist monk Thich Nhat Hanh: "Letting go gives us freedom, and freedom is the only condition for happiness. If, in our heart, we still cling to anything—anger, anxiety, or possessions—we cannot be free."

His suggested mantra is
In, out
Deep, slow
Calm, ease
Smile, release
Present moment, wonderful moment.

Once you settle on your phrases, write them clearly on a piece of paper while saying the words out loud. Place the inspirational note near your bath, in your line of sight, and make sure the paper isn't in danger of falling into the bathtub or catching on fire from a candle. Light your candles while humming or reciting your affirmations.

Place the crystals on the edge of the bathtub as you immerse yourself in the embrace of warm, fragrant water. Let the problems melt away into a fresh, new beginning. Think about your inner agency and take deep breaths as you gaze at each candle, back and forth.

Anchor yourself by taking hold of the smoky quartz, which should neutralize negative vibrations immediately. Press the gem to the base of your spine to stimulate the root chakra; straighten your back and reaffirm your relationship to gravity and Earth. Think of the smoky quartz as pointing to Earth's core, rooting you to this reality as needed for your highest good. If any anxiety arises, remind yourself of the present moment. This crystal makes it easier to meditate and focus on how small some worries actually are, despite the despair you might otherwise feel. Envision your smoky quartz as an amulet of protection shielding you from feeling consumed by life.

Continue to heal your root chakra by picking up the obsidian—not a crystal per se, but a volcanic rock. Press the rock to each heel to empower you to stand firm in tough situations. Think as clearly as possible about the conditions that keep you from moving forward. Obsidian is sometimes referred to as a mirror because of the inner truths it reveals to those who use it. Your conscience might make you think of poor choices that bring you shame, but with the power of the obsidian, convert this anguish and tension into a release of resentment. Forgive yourself and allow the energy stored in your body that you can use to be brave to flow though you and fill you. This is a doorway from fear to freedom.

Grasp and admire the blue kyanite, a welcome pop of color that corresponds to the throat chakra. When the throat chakra is inhibited, people experience self-doubt and shyness, or a fear of being judged. After activating this part of the body, it becomes easier to speak your mind and be confident in your thoughts. However, you'll also head toward a balance of listening as well as talking, and you'll pursue healthy communication with others. Unless the piece is polished, avoid soaking this crystal in water. Instead, hold the kyanite to your throat, appreciating its strong energy and high frequency. Breathe in, breathe out. Promise yourself that you will, in the future, speak your truth with love and respect, and push away those who send negativity in your direction. Pledge to not fall into bad habits when unpleasant moments come your way and to be your authentic self. Feel the freedom of being yourself unabashedly.

Finish with your piece of amethyst, a popular crystal with a memorable lavender hue. Amethyst activates the third eye chakra as well as the crown chakra with its high vibration and protective elements. For the best results, hold the piece firmly in your left hand before first waving it over your brow area (the third eye chakra). Tell yourself that you trust your intuition and vow to clearly see new opportunities on the horizon. You are free to pursue your dreams, and no one can stop you from achieving your goals.

Once you conclude the motions with each crystal, appreciate the individual aesthetic qualities of each piece— show your possessions the love they deserve. Making sure they're safely out of the way, continue your bath by lathering your body in lemongrass soap while basking in the candlelit glow. Repeat your mantras and imagine yourself clean and serene for the rest of the day or night. When you are ready to exit the bath, open the drain, step out, and feel yourself transformed. Feel how you have rejuvenated your self-confidence.

Give yourself a hug in a fresh towel. You should smell amazing from the soap and essential oils, and be internally calm and relaxed. Any baggage you brought with you into the bath is gone, and your mind is finally clear to see the world for its beautiful truth. Treat yourself to another cup of tea and unwind in the way that makes you feel happiest.

Step 2

Find a comfortable place to sit. Let yourself relax but try to be in a position where your spine is straight. Lean back into the couch, chair, or pillow and think about being in alignment with life. When you are sovereign of your domain, you rule it with complete benevolence and you are in total alignment with your world and your life. Bring that truth into your body. Invite yourself to come into proper universal alignment. Take some deep breaths. Prepare to say this phrase, which has resonant, supernatural properties, aloud three times with attention and intention: "Proper universal alignment." As you say this phrase three times, notice how it feels in your body. Notice if it feels like things in your life are repositioning and click into place. These words are like a key in the lock that aligns you with life.

Step 3

Next, do the warrior II yoga pose for strength. Think of yourself as a warrior of the light, except your weapons are love and caring, and your inner strength ensures your victory.

Stand tall and strong with your feet about three to four feet apart. Raise your arms parallel to the floor and reach them out to the sides, shoulder blades open, palms down. Turn your right foot slightly out to the right and your left foot to the left about 90 degrees. Align the left heel and right heel. Turn your left thigh outward and your head facing your left foot. The center of the left kneecap should be in line with the center of the left ankle.

Stand in this position and breathe deeply. Feel the strength in your body and the sovereignty within you.

Step 4

Begin to live your life like a queen or king. Imagine what a beloved and benevolent queen would do in each situation. How would she ensure the good of her people and herself from a place of compassion, caring, and implacable steadiness? Give yourself opportunities each day to practice your sovereignty. Make life choices based upon it, and write about them in your journal at night to affirm the action you're taking to embody the truth of who you are: queen or king of your life.

HOW TO BE YOUR OWN SOVEREIGN

* Think for yourself.

* Practice critical thinking skills.

* Treat yourself with care and regard.

* Share your blessings.

* Lead with love.

* Teach children kindness and confidence.

TURN
LETHARGY
TO
VITALITY

SOMETIMES WE FEEL LIKE WE ARE IN AN energy deficit. We are missing the liveliness and buoyancy we would usually feel. Our exuberance is low, and it could be for many different reasons. It could be because of something that's going on in our career or work life. It could be that we are healing in our emotional world. It could be that there's a conflict in a relationship that's troubling us.

What if you could return to that space of excitement and dynamism? What if you could find more zest for life and see how all of the beautiful moments in your life are actually sparkling and twinkling just for you? In this state, we notice the beauty of life more easily. We see the rays of sunlight glinting off the moisture on the grass outside. We notice how gorgeous the air feels on our skin. We experience the hug we share with a friend deeper in our heart. What if you could bring this level of presence and enjoyment to each moment?

This section is all about enlivening your spirit and helping you turn lethargy into vitality. A key component of vitality is being as present as possible in the moment that is happening right now. The past is over and the future is yet to arrive, but now is the place where your vitality lives.

In this section, we will talk about essential oils that can boost your verve for life. We will examine crystals that can up your level of vivacity. We will talk about plants that can ignite your vigor. We'll engage in a lively and energy-filled bath ritual that will turn up the volume on your own inner wellspring of vital life force. Let's jump into the present moment together and enliven your life in a major way!

Oils to Embrace Life

There are so many wonderful and amazing essential oils that can increase your vitality and energy. These scents and healing compounds can invite your senses to be more awake. They can help your body's metabolic function increase so you literally are receiving more cellular energy. Certain essential oils will lift your mood. Others will increase your ability to enjoy the present moment. The amazing thing about essential oils is that they work on all levels. They work with our physical bodies as medicinal substances, but they also work intimately with our emotional bodies through our senses and the nervous and endocrine systems. Essential oils interact with our hormones and the chemicals that transmit messages throughout our body about what to do and how to feel. They also interact with our nervous system and help it function in a way that's more holistically balanced. Essential oils can also improve mental function overall, specifically cognition and the ability to focus. Essential oils can often provide a doorway to the spiritual and subtle realms. They are powerhouses. Let's tap into their gifts to invigorate our lives today.

The question then becomes, which of the oils do you use? Find out by going through our quick little quiz.

QUESTION 1

When it comes to having the energy levels to do what I like:

1. I have more than enough.

2. I could use a bit more energy but generally have enough to do most things.

3. I only really have the energy to do what I have to get done.

4. Energy? Not unless it's out of a coffee cup.

QUESTION 2

When someone sees me after a single long day on:

1. They don't notice if I might be off.

2. They say I am looking a little tired.

3. They ask if I'm all right.

4. I wouldn't dare leave the house without makeup on those days because my dark eye circles are so prominent.

QUESTION 3

The idea of getting up and going for a walk:

1. Doesn't sound as good as something that really gets my heart pumping.

2. Is interesting, if I can find the right shoes.

3. Sounds okay, but I have a lot to do.

4. Sounds like absolute torture. Where would I drum up the energy?

Add up the numbers of each answer you chose to get your score. For example, if you chose answer 4 for question 1, you will have 4 points for that question.

If Your Score Is 10 to 12

Your vitality needs a serious overhaul. While you aren't actually sick, you are at risk of it. You don't have the energy to work out, prepare great meals, or even really have a lot of fun. What you need are oils that will boost your feelings of well-being and your energy level.

* **2 drops of lavender oil:** This oil is great when you are ill and great when you are not. It boosts the immune system, helps keep you relaxed, and helps beat the symptoms of stress. It won't give you a shock of energy, but it will help you get more done in a day.

* **2 drops of juniper berry oil:** This is a fantastic oil to use on your body to help to boost circulation, reduce water retention, and ease aches and pains. It is uplifting for the mind and can help counter the effects of stress.

If Your Score Is 7 to 9

You have some vital energy and are able to make it through a standard day relatively well. If something out of the ordinary happens, however, or your routine is upset, you are left reeling and trying to cope.

* **2 drops of ginger oil:** This spice oil is very useful when it comes to maintaining vitality. Rub a diluted

mixture on at the first sign of a cold or flu, and you'll be able to short-circuit it. Ginger helps to improve immunity and circulation. It is one of the best oils for treating nervous exhaustion and debility.

* **2 drops of coriander oil:** Coriander oil is not commonly used, but it is excellent for treating neuralgia and nervous exhaustion, boosting immunity, and helping fight general infection.

Again, these are best used applied directly to the body. Ginger can irritate sensitive skin, so use 3 tablespoons mixed with 2 drops of ginger oil and massage on your body. You can apply this mixture to the abdomen if you have an upset stomach; it will increase beneficial warmth in the area.

Coriander oil will also soothe digestion when applied to the abdomen as well as invigorating the senses. Mix 2 drops of coriander oil with 2 tablespoons of carrier oil to the limbs, tops of hands, and feet.

If Your Score Is 5 or 6

You are relatively lively. Wonderful! With a little bit of essential oil support, you will be even more full of life and light.

* **2 drops of violet oil:** This oil is excellent for improving concentration and helping with emotional turmoil.
* **2 drops of basil oil:** This is an excellent nervine tonic and will clear your head quickly. It helps heal the symptoms of a cold or flu and helps rejuvenate the mind.

These two oils have benefits when applied topically, but if all you need is a quick pick-me-up, they'll work well in a diffuser.

If Your Score Is 3 or 4

If you already have loads of energy, the oils you want to focus on are those that help you handle stress and give your mind a boost.

* **2 drops of jasmine oil:** It has a heady scent and is guaranteed to make you feel happier every time you sniff it. It's also a lovely aphrodisiac.
* **2 drops of rose oil:** The rose is not considered the queen of all flowers for nothing. This oil will have you feeling great in next to no time flat and will help you deal with stress more effectively as well.

All the Oils You Should Consider for Vitality

* **For when you just don't have any energy left:** lavender and juniper berry oil.
* **For those who are able to get some things done, but need help:** ginger and coriander oil.
* **For when you just want to take things up a notch:** violet and basil oil.
* **For when you want to maintain perfection:** jasmine and rose oil.

Here are a few more recipes for you.

Vital Exfoliation

1 cup Epsom salts

1 cup coarse sea salt

½ cup baking soda

5 drops juniper berry oil

10 drops ginger oil

Combine the ingredients and put in a sealed container. Allow the mixture to sit overnight so that the scent permeates the salts and soda. To exfoliate your skin, scoop up some of the mixture in your hand and add olive oil to make a paste.

Apply to the skin using slow circular motions, always working up toward the heart. Leave it on for a minute or two, and then rinse off with warm water.

Alternatively, add a handful of the mixture to your bath just prior to you getting in.

Detoxifying Skin Rub

1 cup Epsom salts

1 cup coarse sea salt

5 drops juniper berry oil

5 drops sweet orange oil

5 drops eucalyptus oil

Combine the ingredients and put in a sealed container. Allow the mixture to sit overnight so that the scent permeates the salts. To exfoliate your skin, scoop up some of the mixture in your hand and add olive oil to make a paste.

Apply to the skin using slow circular motions, always working up toward the heart. Leave it on for a minute or two, and then rinse off with warm water.

Alternatively, add a handful of the mixture to your bath just prior to you getting in.

This rub is also extremely useful if you are battling circulation issues and aches and pains.

Endless Energy Carpet Sprinkle

This will scent your carpet to promote vitality and zest for life.

1 cup baking soda

10 drops lime oil

10 drops ginger oil

Mix together the ingredients in a sealed container and store overnight so that the scents can develop. Sprinkle over the bedroom carpet and leave in place for at least two to three hours before vacuuming it up.

Jump and Jive Rejuvenating Body Spray

Use this body spray to increase your vitality and vital life force.

4 ounces of spring water

10 drops grapefruit oil

10 drops geranium oil

Mix together the in a spray bottle and spritz yourself and your clothing liberally.

When it comes to health and vitality, there is no nicer way to do things than with essential oils. They smell great, are highly effective and completely natural, and will not cost a fortune. They offer the perfect vitality solution all around.

All you need to do is to find some that you enjoy using and start incorporating them into your day. It couldn't be simpler, could it?

Vivacious Crystals

Modern-day living takes a lot out of us. It can be difficult to maintain health and vitality with the pace of living that most of us enjoy. Crystals can help you to boost your energy levels and also revitalize your life.

Let's have a look at the many crystals that you can incorporate into your daily life to boost your vitality.

Black Tourmaline

This is a great stone for realigning the energy within your body. It helps to soothe tired and sore muscles and promotes deep sleep and relaxation. It is also a powerful protector when it comes to deflecting negative energy.

Tiger's Eye

It helps to build your confidence, clear up congested systems, and soothe your mind and body. It is a good stone to use when you feel mentally and physically exhausted.

Blue Quartz

This is a pretty stone that helps to stimulate your immune system, helps you break out of harmful habits, and helps you

Condition	Stone	Best Way to Use	Charge With
In need of more restful sleep	Black tourmaline	Keep it on you or under your mattress	Moonlight/sun/ smudge/sand
For physical and mental exhaustion	Tiger's eye	Carry it with you or use it as jewelry	Moonlight/sun/ smudge
General vitality	Blue quartz	Wear it as a necklace	Moonlight/sun/ smudge
Good health	Turquoise	Keep it with you or use as jewelry	Moonlight
Promotes good mental health	Gold	Get yourself a gold chain and possibly gold rings as well	Moonlight
When you need to detox	Diamonds	Wear them in jewelry	Moonlight
When you are recovering from an illness	Diopside	Carry it with you at all times and keep it under your pillow at night.	Moonlight/sun/ smudge

feel naturally more hopeful. It is a good stone to promote overall vitality. It is a very restful stone that also helps to alleviate fear and improve your communication skills.

Turquoise

Be careful that you get real turquoise—a lot of the "turquoise" on the market today is actually dyed howlite.

If you can get the real thing, it is well worth your while. It strengthens all the organs of the body and balances all the energy systems. It helps to soothe an overactive mind and quick temper. It is a powerful protector against negativity in the environment.

It is a stone that can help to heal emotional hurts as well. This is a porous stone, so it is best not to soak it in water.

Gold

Believe it or not, gold does fall into the category of crystal healer. It helps to balance your nervous system and strengthens your immune system. It also balances the body's subtle electrical system and thus is good for overall health and vitality.

Do we really need any more reasons to wear gold jewelry?

Diamond

Of course, if we are springing for gold, then why not some diamonds at the same time? Diamonds are powerful at detoxifying your system. They help to remove negativity and to inspire creativity.

Diopside

If you have been under a lot of stress for a long time, you need to start carrying diopside. It can release stress at a very deep level and help you recover after you have been very ill.

Enlivening Plants and Flowers

Vitality can be defined as a state of being active, energetic, and alive. It is the cultivation of strength, both mental and physical. The more we are energized and alive, the more we can cultivate happiness, love, serenity, and confidence. We can enhance the positive effects of using these herbs with our focused intentions. We can cultivate our intention by having faith in ourselves, our ability to receive benefits, and our trust in the medicinal properties of these herbs.

TULSI, AKA HOLY BASIL *(Ocimum sanctum/Ocimum tenuiflorum)*

This herb has an adaptogenic and stress-relieving effect, but it also can gently energize you. You can use tulsi if you are seeking a gentle boost but not necessarily needing an intense level of concentration. It can be diffused into teas or used in aromatherapy.

GREAT FOR: Energy

SCHISANDRA *(Schisandra chinensis/Schisandra sphenanthera)*

This plant produces flowers that have a stimulating effect on the nervous system. This stimulating effect has been known to produce mental clarity and improve concentration. It strengthens and increases the speed of your reflexes, increases coordination, increases endurance, and aids in memory acquisition and retention. Traditionally, in Chinese medicine, the berries are chewed to produce these desirable effects.

GREAT FOR: Memory, reflexes, endurance

ROSE PETALS *(Rosa)*

This incredibly versatile flower has many uses. Its value and chemical components are still not fully understood. Chinese tradition uses these flowers as well. They are used to increase energy, or chi, as it is referred to in Chinese medicine. These flowers can be dried and used in teas or consumed on their own. Rose petals are also commonly used in aromatherapy and can be infused to create steam.

GREAT FOR: Energy

ROSEMARY *(Rosmarinus officinalis)*

Rosemary herbs can be dried and used in many ways. Teas infused with rosemary are believed to improve cognition and enhance mental clarity. It is also used by soaking the dried herb to create ointments that are great for the skin, but it also works as a method of aromatherapy. Rosemary has been used to treat depression and stress. This is incredibly important to consider when honoring its usefulness in creating vitality. Before moving into a space of strength and creation, we must first remove stress. Rosemary can help you create the clarity and sharpness of cognition needed to push yourself into your space of creativity.

GREAT FOR: Clarity, cognition

BRAHMI *(Bacopa monnieri)*

This herb has been used for centuries as a brain tonic. It is believed to have many cognitive benefits, including enhancing memory. It is also known to relieve stress and anxiety. Herbs that have these serene effects, as well as brain stimulating effects, are some of the best for vitality. Brahmi can be a great herb to use to enhance cognition and stimulate greater intellect. For its cognitive effects, it is best consumed by drying the leaves to make a tea.

GREAT FOR: Memory, intellect, energy

GOTU KOLA *(Centella/Hydrocotyle asiatica)*

This herb is often taken in the form of supplements but was traditionally used in food and drinks. You can find it in capsules, tinctures, and tablets. It can be used in skin creams and body scrubs as well, as it has amazing anti-inflammatory, antiviral, and other beneficial qualities that make it great for your skin. It is another herb that is considered a brain tonic and has been shown to assist the brain in remarkable ways. After using gotu kola for a few weeks, it begins to protect the brain from toxins and mood swings. It encourages the brain to strengthen its structures, by enhancing and stimulating the growth of different parts of neurons. Neuroplasticity is increased, and the brain becomes more capable of protecting itself from harm and enhancing its ability.

GREAT FOR: Memory, learning

GOLDEN ROOT/ROSEROOT/ARCTIC ROOT/ RHODIOLA *(Rhodiola rosea)*

This herb has been employed throughout history to improve the physical body as well as enhance its mental processes. It is believed to help in improving mental processes by first overcoming any mood disturbances, including reactions to stress. It works to improve your mood and allows the body to regulate hormones and neurotransmitters. Bringing the mind into a state of balance is a crucial component of fostering vitality. You can use golden root to enhance your memory and to assist your performance, especially when under stress. It is most commonly used today in herbal supplements. Traditionally, the root was chewed to enhance a person's endurance during long adventures and journeys. It helps you by preventing burnout during a period when you are very physically or mentally active.

GREAT FOR: Stamina, endurance, memory

GINSENG *(Panax ginseng/Panax quinquefolium/Panax notoginseng/Eleutherococcus senticosus)*

There are many different types of ginseng used for various intentions. The root of Siberian ginseng *(Eleutherococcus senticosus)* is used to improve concentration. This is a great herb to substitute for something like coffee or other caffeinated beverages, because it produces a very focused state. It works to improve your concentration much like coffee but without the caffeine crash. One of the simplest and arguably the most efficient methods of using ginseng is brewing ginseng tea. Grind 2 or 3 grams of ginseng root into small pieces or a fine powder. Steep in boiling water for just 5 minutes to create an energizing ginseng tea.

Siberian ginseng has been used for centuries and is extremely useful for warding off the effects of stress. It helps to improve performance mentally, physically, and sexually and can naturally boost your energy levels. It is also useful in boosting the immune system. Be sure that you are getting genuine Siberian ginseng. Supplements containing American or Asian ginseng will often be mistaken for Siberian ginseng, but they have very different benefits.

GREAT FOR: Attention, memory, alertness, energy, focus

CACAO *(Theobroma cacao)*

Cacao is a bean that has been used traditionally to maintain vigor and productivity. Consuming the bean in its raw form is the most effective way of receiving its benefits. Perhaps one of cacao's most surprising ways of assisting in overall vitality is its nutritional value. This bean contains more than three hundred components that can assist your body in its overall health and functioning, including minerals like magnesium, iron, zinc, copper, and calcium, which are essential for the body to absorb nutrients and function properly. These minerals can help to alleviate signs of fatigue and low energy. Magnesium in particular is an important mineral for experiencing a balanced mood and feeling relaxed. Raw cacao is also considered an antioxidant that can allow you to experience some relief from the natural effects of stress and aging and help improve longevity. The way cacao can assist you in your love life is also translatable

a bath infusion by stuffing the mugwort into a muslin bag, closing it tight, and dropping it into the water. This should act like a giant teabag for your bath. Like the essential oils, the mugwort infusion will make you feel sleepy and ready for bed after it soaks into your pores, but you will enjoy increased vivacity the next day.

Set the tone for your soak by writing down a prayer, affirmation, or mantra that refreshes your spirit. It can be as simple as "I'm ready for any challenge," "Nothing can stop me," or "I embody strength." Be confident with your wishes if you choose to make a wish. Trust that this phrase or set of phrases emboldens you to face the road ahead. Say the phrases out loud as you write them down and put the piece of paper within your line of sight.

Light a purple candle, which will represent the aura you're hoping to project from your crown chakra. The royal color will boost confidence and may help you to feel not like just a king or queen but like a god or goddess.

Start out with your piece of luminous moonstone, moving it back and forth in the glowing light of the purple candle, so you can appreciate its opalescence. Moonstone has a feminine energy and is primarily associated with the Greek goddess Aphrodite. If it isn't obvious from the name, moonstone is influenced by the lunar cycle and can be used whether the moon is waxing or waning, but it is most potent during a full moon. Irrespective of your gender, let the feminine stone massage your sensitive emotional nature and maternal instincts. Elongate your body and rub the moonstone over your solar plexus, located between the navel and the top of the sternum. Without unblocking your solar plexus chakra, you won't be able to awaken any of the upper chakras—everything is connected in the chakra system. Affirm your joyous sense of self and your desire to live in the present moment. Shed the trappings of apathy and ennui that may have held you back thus far.

Slowly hover the moonstone up over your heart and let it become one with the organ's rhythm. Forgive yourself for any mistakes like infidelity, withholding of emotion, or not being present and kind to yourself. In this moment, you are showing up for yourself and your future. From this point forward you can pledge to offer a more vibrant version of yourself to the ones who need it most. Set the intention to quell anger and aggression toward yourself and to be gentle and open.

Now roll the moonstone over your third eye chakra and picture a new beginning for yourself, fixating deeply on what a new beginning means for you. Conjure up what you want to see in your surroundings and let those desires take the reins in your mind's eye. Visualize a positive course of action in times of crisis; tell yourself that you have the infinite agency of a goddess.

Move on to the howlite. Your opaque white rock should have gray lines streaking across the surface. Place it on your brow center (your third eye chakra and sixth sense). Take deep breaths in and out, picturing the air passing through your nostrils. For those who have trouble sleeping, howlite is remarkably powerful against insomnia. The next time your head meets the pillow, you'll be bathed in a serene glow. It helps remove paranoia, bringing you back to reality. Focusing all your energy in the center of your forehead, extract the feeling that you have always been powerful, reminding yourself of the earlier goddess vision. Connect the howlite to your divine center at the top of your head, clearing the crown chakra.

Amethyst is as potent as it is popular; finding the crystal in large quantities is easy. Its deep purple aura works on the third eye and crown chakras. Bathing with a piece of amethyst in the glow of a purple candle will, according to some, "sharpen the sixth sense." In Chinese culture, tradition holds that this jewel aids lawyers in winning lawsuits and portends success in business. It also plays an important role in the Greek myth of Dionysus, the god of wine, and thus protects against intoxication. Engaging with amethyst supposedly prevents you from embarrassing yourself under the influence, no matter how much you've had to drink. More prudent drinkers can use the crystal to ward off accidental drunkenness while enjoying the taste of wine: without headache, nausea, or hangover. In a modern context, this meaning extends to drugs. Amethyst may fortify a person's strength to abstain from drugs altogether.

Use the amethyst piece to balance your aura and clear away negative thoughts weighing you down. Rub it on your forehead, imagining violet cosmic rays filling your head to the very top. Let the rays bring you insight to ultimately enliven your being. Visualize your mental stress rising from your head like a cloud of fog. Think about your physical brain occupying your skull; picture the gray matter beaming violet, the two halves flickering alternately and vibration trickling down your spinal cord. Envision your pulsing nerves sending the energy from top to bottom, and bottom to top. Your whole body is connected by tiny beads. Sit up in the bath and think of a string pulling you from your tailbone to the ceiling.

Like amethyst, clear quartz clears and rebalances the crown chakra. Often, the pieces come carved in a wand or arrow shape, which you may point toward you to direct the universe's energy into your body and into the bathtub. Think of this as a divine power cord, charging you to connect with your higher power. Appreciate the weight of your wand. Ponder briefly how large a piece of clear quartz would be if it weighed as much as your body. Strive to have your lingering problems weigh less than the crystal in your hand.

After the crystals have worked their magic on your chakras, put them aside and lather your body with whatever soap you enjoy. Scrub your skin of all the toxins and dead cells accumulated from work and play. Take a few deeper breaths and step out of the tub, swaddling yourself in a fresh towel. Blow out your candle and put your crystals in a safe place for next time, or under your pillow for vivid dreams.

Sparkle Ritual

Do you jump out of bed in the morning ready for the day, or do you have to drag yourself up and get a cup of coffee to start the day off? Vitality is something that we seem to have less and less of as we get older and busier.

The great news is that you can revive your flagging energy levels if you are willing to work at it. It may take some time to accomplish, but you can regain the energy that you had when you were a teenager.

Some Interesting Facts about Your Metabolism

Did you know that your metabolism is responsible for your energy levels throughout the day? The more effective your metabolism is, the better it will be at producing the energy that you want.

Here are some fascinating facts:

* Your basal metabolic rate is what is mostly responsible for how much energy your body uses when you are sedentary. This is the absolute minimum energy that your body needs to survive.

* Muscles require more energy, so one of the best ways to increase your basal metabolic rate naturally is by working on toning your muscles and getting them into good shape.

* If you do not eat enough food on a given day, your body's metabolic rate slows to reduce energy expenditure. Therefore, starvation diets do not work.
* Fluctuations in blood sugar levels can also play havoc with your metabolic rate and your energy levels. Keeping your blood sugar levels constant by following a healthy eating plan with plenty of protein and only a little sugar will ensure that you always have enough energy to do what you need.
* Eating breakfast in the morning gets your metabolism off to a good start. This is why you should never skip breakfast. Choose a high-protein breakfast to power up your morning.
* How much quality sleep you get at night can also influence your metabolic rate. A minimum of eight hours is recommended.

Now that you know a bit more about energy and your metabolism, let's explore some herbs that can help you naturally improve your vitality.

How to Naturally Improve Your Vitality

The first step is always to start implementing better eating habits and incorporating exercise into your daily routine. The human body was never designed to be stationary for hours every day, and it certainly was not designed to sit in one position all day. If you are truly serious about vitality, you need to start living an active lifestyle.

It's not just your diet that needs to be overhauled. You need to ensure that you get at least eight hours of sleep every night and that you take time off regularly to rest and recharge.

We will use the following plants in our ritual to regain your vitality:

Wheatgrass

Adding more greens to your daily diet is essential. A wheatgrass shot in the morning is a fantastic way to get you started off properly for the day. It contains high levels of vitamins and minerals, chlorophyll, and amino acids and will give you a jolt of energy. You can juice it or incorporate it into a healthy smoothie.

Cordyceps

This is a type of mushroom native to Asia and has been touted as a cure-all. Scientific research points to it having antioxidant properties as well as significant anti-inflammatory properties. It has also shown promising results in the treatment of cancer.

For general vitality, though, it is important because it helps rev up ATP production in the body. ATP is essential for the proper storage of energy in the system.

In fact, it is so effective that Chinese athletes used it during the 1993 Olympic games to improve their performance. While not illegal, the extract was so effective that they were tested for performance-enhancing drugs. That is how it was discovered that they had used the extract.

Ashwagandha

This is an adaptogen that has long been used in Ayurvedic medicine as a tonic. It has been prized as a healer and is said to improve immunity, increase energy and vitality, and stave off neurological issues.

Its value here is that it supports the thyroid and the adrenal glands. It is one of the best herbs to use if you are suffering from adrenal fatigue due to long-term exposure to stress. Its regulating effect on the thyroid will help stave off fatigue.

It is a nightshade plant, so if you have an intolerance to this family of plants, as many do, omit it.

Sparkle Ritual to Start Your Day

We are often advised to have a winding-down ritual at night. This lets the body know that it is time for sleep. It makes sense then to have a morning ritual to let your body know that it is time to get up and get active, doesn't it?

Step 1

Forget the snooze button. The snooze button might easily be one of the worst inventions ever. That extra 10 minutes of sleep does you zero good and really only damages your sleep cycle.

From now on, banish the snooze button. In fact, start working on getting rid of the alarm clock as well. If you find that you still need it to wake you in the morning, it means you are not sleeping enough. Try going to bed 15 minutes earlier at night. Keep moving your bedtime back until you can easily awaken at the right time without your alarm going off.

Step 2

Have a glass of warm water with the juice of half a lemon in it. This will help to alkalize your system and promote detoxification. If you are up to it, stir in ½ teaspoon of cayenne pepper to jumpstart your metabolism and help boost your cardiovascular system.

Step 3

Start the day with the yoga sequence called the sun salutation or salute to the sun. You can find some great videos online that you can follow every day until you have the sequence down perfectly.

This is actually a series of poses that gently and effectively stretch every muscle in your body. They help boost circulation and lymphatic drainage, and you will find them extremely effective in giving you the energy that you need for the day ahead.

Step 4

Enjoy a wheatgrass juice shot or make a smoothie with wheatgrass, cordyceps extract, and ashwaganda extract. Combine in the blender with frozen kale, berries, and the nut milk, rice milk, or juice of your choice.

Step 5

Take a walk outdoors in the sunlight. If you have a garden, spend at least 5 to 10 minutes in it in the morning. If you like, you could perform the sun salutation in the garden once you have the hang of it. If you don't have a garden, just go outside and enjoy the sun and fresh air.

The Mood Book

Step 6

Set your intention for the day. Do this by creating a journal especially for this purpose. Start out by listing five things for which you are grateful. It is important to do this in the morning, even if you also do it at night, because it helps you focus on things that you already have before you start your day.

Next, make a note of your intention for the day. This is very similar to an affirmation, and its purpose is the same: to get you in the right frame of mind.

Choose something positive, like "I have boundless energy. I feel vital and blissful and can cope with any challenges that might present themselves. I feel vital energy flowing through my veins that strengthen and energize every part of my being."

Step 7

Take a minute after you finish writing to sit calmly with your eyes closed. Breathe in for a count of five and, as you do so, visualize an energizing white light entering your body and spreading to every part of it. Breathe in deeply and with every breath take in more of this energy until you feel it in every part of your body.

When you feel suitably energized, open your eyes again and start to get breakfast ready. It is important to have a healthy breakfast that will give you plenty of energy for the morning ahead. If you made a smoothie earlier and would like that to be your breakfast, then add a high-quality vegan protein powder to the mix and a bit of optional flaxseed or evening primrose oil.

Ditch the sugary cereals and focus more on protein and a bit of slow-release carbs such as oats. You might have some full-fat, organic, unsweetened Greek or sheep's milk yogurt. Mix in some fresh fruit to add some flavor, and consider adding natural coconut flakes as well. The healthy fat in the morning with satiate you for longer as you go about your day.

Step 8

Get dressed and consider spritzing your clothing with some peppermint linen spray. Test it in an inconspicuous place to make sure the colors won't run and the fabric won't be damaged. (This spray is not suitable for dry-clean-only clothing.)

As an alternative, you can spritz some of the linen spray into the air and walk into it—much the same way as with perfume. This will leave a delicate scent without causing too much damage.

Consider making your own linen spray. It is very simple to do and will be a lot more beneficial than the typical commercial brands that use synthetic chemical ingredients that could harm your health, rather than improve it.

Pure essential oil has a wide range of therapeutic benefits and none of the nasty side-effects of harsh chemicals. Peppermint oil is particularly useful because it helps to clear out the cobwebs in the brain and keep you awake.

Making Your Own Linen Spray

With just three ingredients, it does not get much simpler than this.

**20 drops therapeutic grade organic peppermint
essential oil**

**250 milliliters distilled water (plain tap water
will do in a pinch)**

**50 milliliters cheap vodka (optional; helps the oils to
disperse in the water and will evaporate quickly)**

Mix everything together and put it in a spray bottle.
Shake every time you use it and store it in a cool cupboard
between uses.

An alternative is to put a few drops of peppermint oil
into the rinse water after washing your clothing.

I will be the first to admit that this ritual does have quite
a few steps. You can adjust this ritual as you'd like to suit
your schedule. However, it is nice to be able to take some
time in the morning to ease yourself into the day calmly, so
do consider following all of the steps.

ACKNOWLEDGMENTS

I'm incredibly grateful to the talented team at Sterling Ethos. Again and again, they produce beautiful, high-quality, engaging books that I get the wonderful privilege of writing. Infinite thanks to Kate Zimmerman, my fabulous editor, who helps give birth to my dreams. She is a dream to work with, and it is a gift to learn from her. Gratitude to Ashten Luna for her exemplary editorial prowess. Thank you so much to the talented designers who made this book so beautiful. Hugs and recognition to the sales, distribution, and marketing teams at Sterling. I continue to be in awe when I see one of my books in Barnes & Noble, Whole Foods, Costco, BJ's, and all the other amazing stores where you place them.

I am incredibly blessed to have the nicest, most experienced, most effective literary agent I could ever dream of for this book. Lisa Hagan is an example of excellence in her field, and I am privileged to work with her.

I have been blessed with an amazing network of powerful women in this industry whom I also call friends. My dear friend and marketer extraordinaire Jamie Eslinger of Spire Marketing gets me in front of all the right people so I get to share my ideas and live my life's purpose with joy.

None of this would be possible without my stupendously supportive family and my magnificently kind friends. Through time spent together, phone calls, text messages, emails, you are all there and buoy my spirits and make my life worth living.

REFERENCES

"About Our Kava Kava." Root of Happiness. https://rootofhappinesskava.com/pages/about-kava-kava, accessed March 20, 2018.

Alban, Deane. "How Gotu Kola Benefits Your Brain, Mood, and Memory." Be Brain Fit, https://bebrainfit.com/gotu-kola-benefits-brain, Accessed March 20, 2018.

Ali, Babar, et al. "Essential Oils Used in Aromatherapy: A Systemic Review." ScienceDirect. July 10, 2015. https://www.sciencedirect.com/science/article/pii/S2221169115001033, accessed April 4, 2018.

Bar-Sela, G., et al. "The Medical Use of Wheatgrass: Review of the Gap between Basic and Clinical Applications." *Mini Reviews in Medicinal Chemistry* 15, no. 12 (2015): 1002–1010. https://www.ncbi.nlm.nih.gov/pubmed/26156538, accessed April 7, 2018.

"Cacao." Happy Herb Company. http://happyherbcompany.com/cacao, accessed March 20, 2018.

"Calamus Root." Happy Herb Company. http://happyherbcompany.com/calamus-root, accessed March 20, 2018.

Chevalier, Freedom. "Marijuana Tea Benefits, Effects, Recipe, and Dosages." Nugg, March 15, 2016. http://blog.getnugg.com/marijuana-tea-benefits.

Cho, Mi-Yeon, et al. "Effects of Aromatherapy on the Anxiety, Vital Signs, and Sleep Quality of Percutaneous Coronary Intervention Patients in Intensive Care Units."

Evidence-Based Complementary and Alternative Medicine, 2013. https://www.ncbi.nlm.nih.gov/pmc/articles/ PMC3588400, accessed April 4, 2018.

"Cocoa Beans." Herb Wisdom. https://www.herbwisdom. com/herb-cocoa.html, accessed March 20, 2018.

"Emblica officinalis." Examine.com. https://examine.com/ supplements/emblica-officinalis, accessed March 20, 2018.

"15 Herbs to Increase Your Feelings of Happiness (Got to Love #8)." NaturalON. https://naturalon.com/15-herbs-to-increase-your-feelings-of-happiness-got-to-love-8, accessed March 20, 2018.

Fix Editors. "Creative Ways to Use the Herbs Grown in Your Garden." Food and Wine, June 22, 2017. http:// www.foodandwine.com/fwx/creative-ways-use-herbs-grown-your-garden.

Goldman, Ellen. *As Others See Us: Body Movement and the Art of Successful Communication.* London: Taylor and Francis, 2003.

Groves, Maria Noel. "Herbal Teas for Peace and Serenity." Storey, http://www.storey.com/article/herbal-tea-peace-serenity, accessed March 20, 2018.

Hall, Judy. *The Crystal Bible.* Cincinnati: Walking Stick Press, 2003.

Hall, Judy. *Crystals: How to Use Crystals and Their Energy to Enhance Your Life.* London: Hay House Publishers. 2015.

"Herbs That May Increase Self-Confidence." Mystical

Magical Herbs, December 17, 2014. https://
mysticalmagicalherbs.com/2014/12/17/herbs-that-may-
increase-self-confidence.

"Kanna." Smokable Herbs. https://www.smokableherbs.com/
kanna-sceletium-tortuosum, accessed March 20, 2018.

Lawless, Julia. *The Encyclopedia of Essential Oils*. New York:
HarperCollins, 2002.

Lembo, Margaret Ann. *Chakra Awakening*. Woodbury,
MN: Llewellyn Publications, 2011.

Leonard, Jayne. "20 Unusual Ways to Use Rosemary That
Goes [*sic*] Way Beyond Cooking." Natural Living Ideas,
May 9, 2016. http://www.naturallivingideas.com/20-
ways-to-use-rosemary.

Lilly, Simon, and Sue Lilly. *The Essential Crystal Handbook*.
London: Duncan Baird Publishers, 2006.

"Matricaria Chamomilla (German Chamomile)." *Alternative
Medicine Review*, vol. 13, no. 1 (2008): 58–62.

Mattioli, L., C. Funari, and M. Perfumi. "Effects of
Rhodiola Rosea L. Extract on Behavioural and
Physiological Alterations Induced by Chronic Mild
Stress in Female Rats." *Journal of Psychopharmacology*
23, no. 2 (2009). http://journals.sagepub.com/doi/
abs/10.1177/0269881108089872.

McCaffrey, R., D. J. Thomas, and A. O. Kinzelman. "The
Effects of Lavender and Rosemary Essential Oils on
Test-Taking Anxiety among Graduate Nursing Students,"

Holistic Nursing Practice 23, no. 2 (2009), 88–93, doi: 10.1097/HNP.0b013e3181a110aa.

McCutcheon, Jade Rosina. *Awakening the Performing Body.* Amsterdam: Editions Rodopi, 2008.

McIntyre, Anne. "Are There Herbs for Low Self Esteem?" Anne McIntyre Herbal Medicine and Ayurveda. http://annemcintyre.com/books/articles/herbs-for-low-self-esteem, accessed March 20, 2018.

Morgan, Diane. *Gemlore: Ancient Secrets and Modern Myths from the Stone Age to the Rock Age.* Westport, CT: ABC-CLIO, 2008.

Moss, Mark, and Lorraine Oliver. "Plasma 1,8-cineole correlates with cognitive performance following exposure to rosemary essential oil aroma." *Therapeutic Advances in Psychopharmacology* 2, no. 3 (2012): 103–113. http://journals.sagepub.com/doi/abs/10.1177/2045125312436573.

Neufeld, Jessica. "Herbal Teas Under the Microscope." *Organic Gardening* 58, no. 5 (2011): 74–75.

Nhat Hanh, Thich. *The Heart of the Buddha's Teaching.* New York: Broadway Books, 1998.

Nhat Hanh, Thich. *Present Moment Wonderful Moment: Mindfulness Verses for Daily Living.* Berkeley, CA: Parallax Press, 1990.

"Online Herbal Encyclopedia of Knowledge." Cloverleaf Farm. http://www.cloverleaffarmherbs.com, accessed March 20, 2018.

Panossian, Alexander, and Georg Wikman. "Effects of Adaptogens on the Central Nervous System and the Molecular Mechanisms Associated with Their Stress-Protective Activity." *Pharmaceuticals (Basel)* 3, no. 1 (2010): 188–224. https://www.ncbi.nlm.nih.gov/pmc/articles/PMC3991026/, accessed April 7, 2018.

Patel, Sanjay R., et al. "Association between Reduced Sleep and Weight Gain in Women." *American Journal of Epidemiology* 164, no. 10 (2006): 947–954. https://academic.oup.com/aje/article/164/10/947/162270, accessed April 4, 2018.

Raether, Edie. *Sex for the Soul: Seven Secrets of Sensual Intimacy for Spiritual Ecstasy.* Holly Springs, NC: Performance Plus Publishing, 2004.

Ramazanov, Zakir, and Musa Abidoff. "Rhodiola Rosea: Golden Root for Human Health." Nutraceuticals World, January 3, 2000. https://www.nutraceuticalsworld.com/issues/2000-03/view_features/rhodiola-rosea-golden-root-for-human-health.

Raybould, Daisy. "Top 5 Herbs for Glowing and Gorgeous Skin." Mind Body Green, March 2, 2012. https://www.mindbodygreen.com/0-4151/Top-5-Herbs-For-Glowing-Gorgeous-Skin.html.

Rich, Penny. *Practical Aromatherapy.* Bath, England: Parragon Publishing, 1994.

Sacrednailia. "Romantic Love and Raw Chocolate Connection Explained with 'Chocolate-Love Science.'" Sacred Chocolate, February 4, 2015. https://

sacredchocolate.wordpress.com/2015/02/04/what-raw-chocolate-has-in-common-with-love.

Salina, Sandi. "Chamomile's Calming Properties May Be Real." *Environmental Nutrition* 38, no. 2 (2015): 3.

Shiva, Shahram. "Hush Don't Say Anything to God: Passionate Poems of Rumi." Freemont, CA: Jain Publishing, 2000.

Shusterman, Richard. "Body Consciousness and Performance: Somaesthetics East and West." *Journal of Aesthetics and Art Criticism* 67, no. 2 (2009): 133–145.

Singh, Narendra, et al. "An Overview on Ashwagandha: A Rasayana (Rejuvenator) of Ayurveda." *African Journal of Traditional, Complementary, and Alternative Medicines* 8, no. 5 (suppl.) (2011): 208–213. https://www.ncbi.nlm.nih.gov/pmc/articles/PMC3252722, accessed April 7, 2018.

"Sleep Deprivation and Deficiency." National Heart, Lung, and Blood Institute. https://www.nhlbi.nih.gov/health-topics/sleep-deprivation-and-deficiency, Accessed April 4, 2018.

"*Terminalia arjuna* Benefits, How to Use, Research, Side Effects." Easy Ayurveda. https://easyayurveda.com/2014/12/15/terminalia-arjuna-benefits-how-to-use-research-side-effects, accessed March 20, 2018.

Tuli, Hardeep S., Sardul S. Sandhu, and A. K. Sharma. "Pharmacological and Therapeutic Potential of Cordyceps with Special Reference to Cordycepin." *3 Biotech* 4, no. 1 (2014): 1–12. https://www.ncbi.nlm.nih.gov/pmc/articles/PMC3909570/, accessed April 7, 2018.

"Using Brahmi Leaves Benefits, Preparation, and Recipes."
Nootriment. https://nootriment.com/brahmi-leaves,
accessed March 20, 2018.

Walker, Meadow. "Herbs That May Increase Self-
Confidence." Mystical Magical Herbs, December 17,
2014. https://mysticalmagicalherbs.com/2014/12/17/
herbs-that-may-increase-self-confidence.

"What Is Euphoria?" Fogut. https://fogut.com/euphoric-
high-herbs, accessed March 20, 2018.

Whittemore, Frank. "How to Use Dried Ginseng Root."
Livestrong, October 3, 2017. https://www.livestrong.com/
article/95483-use-dried-ginseng-root.

NOTES

Notes

Notes

Notes

Notes

Notes

Notes

INDEX

Note: Page numbers in parentheses indicate non-contiguous references. Page numbers in **bold** indicate summaries of subject's characteristics and uses.

ABOUT THE AUTHOR

Amy Leigh Mercree's motto is "Live joy. Be kind. Love unconditionally." She counsels women and men in the underrated art of self-love to create happier lives. Amy is a bestselling author, media personality, and medical intuitive. Mercree speaks internationally focusing on kindness, joy, and wellness.

Mercree is the bestselling author of *The Spiritual Girl's Guide to Dating: Your Enlightened Path to Love, Sex, and Soul Mates, A Little Bit of Chakras: An Introduction to Energy Healing, Joyful Living: 101 Ways to Transform Your Spirit and Revitalize Your Life, The Chakras and Crystals Cookbook: Juices, Sorbets, Smoothies, Salads, and Crystal Infusions to Empower Your Energy Centers, The Compassion Revolution: 30 Days of Living from the Heart, A Little Bit of Meditation, Essential Oils Handbook, Apple Cider Vinegar Handbook,* and *A Little Bit of Mindfulness: Staying Present in a Hectic World.*

Mercree has been featured in *Glamour, Women's Health, Inc, Shape, The Huffington Post, Soul and Spirit Magazine, Your Tango.com,* Mind Body Green, CBS, NBC, and many more.

Check out AmyLeighMercree.com for articles, picture quotes, and quizzes. Mercree is fast becoming one of the most quoted women on the web. See what all the buzz is about @ AmyLeighMercree on Twitter, Snapchat, and Instagram.

To download your free Mood Book toolkit and illuminate your spirit with fun right now, go to www. amyleighmercree.com/moodbooktoolkit; password MOODBOOK.